SYMMETRY AS THE FUNDAMENT OF SOUND CREATION

Paul Amrod

SYMMETRY AS THE FUNDAMENT OF SOUND CREATION

SYMMETRIE ALS GRUNDPRINZIP DER KLANGSCHÖPFUNG

Bibliografische Information der Deutschen Nationalbibliothek
Die Deutsche Nationalbibliothek verzeichnet diese Publikation in der
Deutschen Nationalbibliografie; detaillierte bibliografische Daten sind
im Internet unter http://dnb.d-nb.de abrufbar.

978-3-95983-587-9 (Paperback)
978-3-95983-588-6 (Hardcover)

© 2019 Schott Music GmbH & Co. KG, Mainz

www.schott-buch.com

Umschlagmotiv: https://pixabay.com/en/fractal-stars-universe-background-764928/
German Translation: Mats Hunger-Heimer
Lektorat: Carolin Bruhn
Layout: Bernadette Meessen

Alle Rechte vorbehalten. Nachdruck in jeder Form sowie die Wiedergabe
durch Fernsehen, Rundfunk, Film, Bild- und Tonträger oder Benutzung für
Vorträge, auch auszugsweise, nur mit Genehmigung des Verlags.

TABLE OF CONTENTS

SYMMETRICAL AXES, SEQUENCES and SYMMETRIES in PITCH RELATIONSHIP   7

1) THEORY OF HARMONY THROUGH THE PATTERNING OF SYMMETRICAL AXES   9

2) THE EMERGENCE OF THE STARTING POINT AS A SYMMETRICAL ROOT   23

3) THESAURUS OF TRANPOSABLE UNEQUALLY DISTRIBUTED MODES   30

4) THE APPLICATIONS OF MODES WITH MULTIPLE SYMMETRIES   38

5) FOUR METHODS OF MODAL EXTENSION   45

6) A NEW DODECAPHONY THROUGH THE USAGE OF POLYMODALITY AND ADJACENT MODES   74

7) THESAURUS OF SYMMETRICAL TWELVE-TONE ROWS   80

8) THE USAGE OF MUSICAL UNITIES   94

9) THESAURUS OF MUSICAL UNITIES IN SCALE FORM   111

9a) MUSICAL UNITIES and SEQUENCES AS SYNTHETIC SYMMETRIES   113

10) AN ALTERNATIVE METHOD FOR CONTROLLED TRANSPOSITION THROUGH THE USAGE OF ORDERED INVERSIONS AND SYMMETRICAL GENERATION   120

11) INVERSIONS FROM THE DISTANCE OF A TRITONE AND IN GRADUATING MAJOR THIRDS   125

12) CONTROLLING THE DYNAMICS OF TRANSPOSITION THROUGH THE NATURE OF THE OVERTONE SERIES   133

13) THE POLYMODAL MARRIAGE OF AN ORDERED INVERTED ENVIRONMENT   140

14) TONALITY and MODALITY   149

15) THE APPLICATION OF THE THEORY IN THE WORLD OF MICROTONICS   165

INHALTSVERZEICHNIS

SYMMETRISCHE ACHSEN, SEQUENZEN UND SYMMETRIEN
ALS GRUNDLAGE DER NOTENVERHÄLTNISSE — 7

1) HARMONIELEHRE – THEORIE DER MUSTER SYMMETRISCHER ACHSEN — 9

2) DIE ETABLIERUNG EINES GRUNDTONS ALS SYMMETRISCHE WURZEL — 23

3) SAMMLUNG TRANSPONIERBARER UNGLEICH VERTEILTER MODI — 30

4) DIE ANWENDUNG VON MODI MIT MEHREREN SYMMETRIEN — 38

5) VIER METHODEN MODALER ERWEITERUNG — 45

6) EINE NEUE DODEKAPHONIE DURCH POLYMODALITÄT UND SICH ERGÄNZENDE MODI — 74

7) SAMMLUNG SYMMETRISCHER ZWÖLFTONREIHEN — 80

8) DIE ANWENDUNG MUSIKALISCHER EINHEITEN — 88

9) SAMMLUNG MUSIKALISCHER EINHEITEN IN SKALENFORM — 105

9a) MUSIKALISCHE EINHEITEN UND SEQUENZEN ALS SYNTHETISCHE SYMMETRIEN — 107

10) EINE ALTERNATIVE METHODE ZUR KONTROLLIERTEN TRANSPOSITION DURCH DEN GEBRAUCH GEORDNETER UMKEHRUNG UND SYMMETRISCHER GENERIERUNG — 114

11) UMKEHRUNGEN DER DISTANZ EINES TRITONUS UND FORTSCHREITENDER GROSSER TERZEN — 119

12) KONTROLLE DER DYNAMIK VON TRANSPOSITIONEN DURCH DIE NATUR DER OBERTONREIHE — 127

13) POLYMODALITÄT UND DIE GEORDNETE UMKEHRUNGSUMGEBUNG — 134

14) TONALITÄT UND MODALITÄT — 143

15) DIE ANWENDUNG DER THEORIE IN DER WELT DER MIKROTONIE — 159

PREFACE

SYMMETRICAL AXES, SEQUENCES and SYMMETRIES in PITCH RELATIONSHIP

In the upcoming theory the phrase "symmetrical axis" is derived from perfect divisions of an octave. In this sense symmetrical because these divisions create equal noninvertible entities. The interval the tritone divides the octave into two equal parts and is in itself noninvertible. The augmented triad divides the octave into three equal parts and is as well noninvertible. These are our two symmetrical axes. The other symmetrical axes for example, the diminished seventh chord or the whole-tone scale, possible in the twelve note well-tempered system are multiples of these two symmetrical axes.

VORWORT

SYMMETRISCHE ACHSEN, SEQUENZEN und SYMMETRIEN als GRUNDLAGE der NOTENVERHÄLTNISSE

Die folgende Musiktheorie basiert auf der Symmetrie von vollkommen regelmäßig unterteilten Oktaven. Der „Tritonus" unterteilt die Oktave in zwei gleiche Teile und ist in sich selbst unumkehrbar. Der übermäßige Dreiklang unterteilt die Oktave in drei gleiche Teile und ist in sich selbst ebenfalls unumkehrbar. Das sind unsere zwei Symmetrieachsen. Andere symmetrische Achsen, die es im wohltemperierten Zwölf-Ton-System gibt, zum Beispiel der verminderte Septakkord oder die Ganzton-Tonleiter, sind Vielfache dieser symmetrischen Achsen.

EXAMPLE 1

The theory is focused on the generation of modes.

Diese Theorie hat die Erschaffung von Modi zum Ziel,

EXAMPLE 2

Also we have the usage of sequential melodic figures based on these symmetrical axes

ebenso Sequenzen auf Symmetrieachsen und

EXAMPLE 3

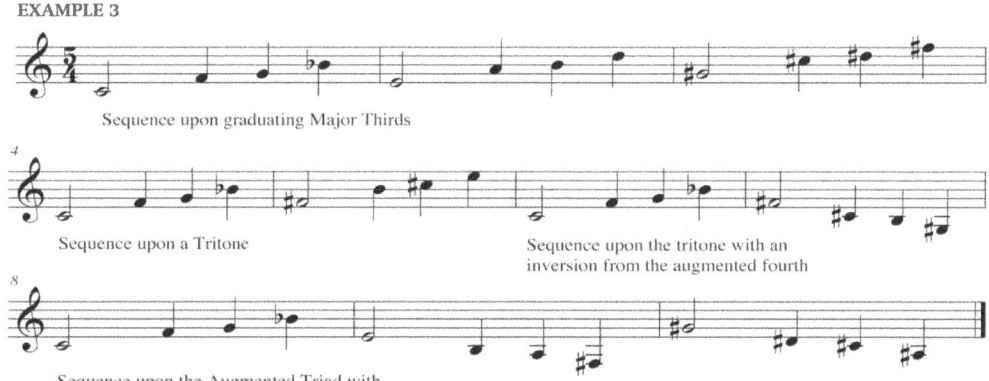

as well as symmetries based on equal intervallic distance from a given pitch.

Klangfiguren, die auf symmetrischer Basis entstehen.

EXAMPLE 4

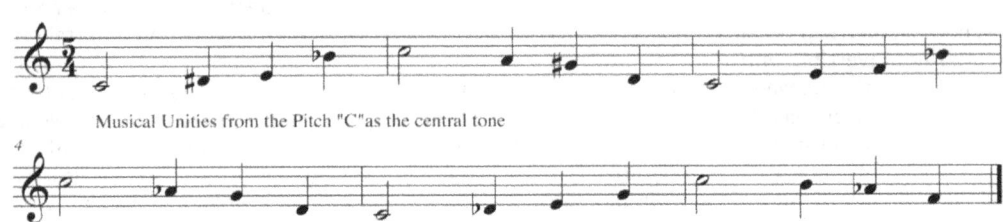

Musical Unities from the Pitch "C" as the central tone

In the last chapter we will adventure into the world of microtonics where other divisions of the octave are possible. For example perhaps the division of 15 pitches equally dividing the octave. We can therefore receive another prime numerical symmetrical axis of 5 divisions.

Because we are dividing the octave with these symmetrical axes the building of modes will be within an octave. However the building of intervallic symmetries does not have this boundary. Intervallic symmetry I will be describing later as a method of creating various musical unities. These are perfect inversions from a given pitch. With these basic premises we will begin the further clarification of the function of symmetry in music.

The usage of rhythmical symmetries will not be discussed however throughout music there are many wonderful methods approaching their usage.

Im letzten Kapitel machen wir einen Ausflug in die abenteuerliche Welt der Mikrotonalität, in der weitere Aufteilungen der Oktave möglich sind. Hier gibt es zum Beispiel die Möglichkeit, die Oktave in 15 Töne gleichen Abstands zu gliedern. Daraus kann wiederum eine Symmetrieachse basierend auf der Primzahl 5 gebildet werden.

Da wir die Oktave symmetrisch teilen, wird sich der Aufbau von Modi auf den Raum einer Oktave beziehen. Die Bildung intervallbezogener Symmetrien ist jedoch nicht auf diesen Vorgang begrenzt.

In einem weiteren Kapitel werden Intervallsymmetrien als Methode zur Schaffung einer Vielzahl von „musikalischen Einheiten" näher beschrieben.

Diese Einheiten haben die gleichen Intervallabstände eines beliebigen Tones.

Die bis dahin dargestellten Grundvoraussetzungen ermöglichen uns in der Folge eine weitgehende Klärung der Funktion der Symmetrie in der Musik.

Der Gebrauch rhythmischer Symmetrien wird hier nicht behandelt werden.

Allerdings gibt es viele interessante Methoden zur Untersuchung dieses Bereiches.

1) THEORY OF HARMONY THROUGH THE PATTERNING OF SYMMETRICAL AXES

Through my explorations into the harmony at the beginning of the 20th Century and my passion for the hard-bop modern jazz from 1955 to the present, I have formulated a new concept as an alternative to the "equal importance" of notes, as found in dodecaphony.

Through the observance of symmetrical axes I began to pattern tritones following typical serial methods. For Example *C-F#, E-A#, Eb-A, Bb-E, Ab-D, A-D#*. This I will utilize for the building of the first row. Then one can, like a twelve-tone row, invert the row. This results in another row of seven tritones which are structurally related. *C-F#, Ab-D, A-D#, D-G#, E-A#, Eb-A*. At this point I distribute pitches around the symmetrical axes and develop modes for a melodical and harmonical resource. In other words each modal resource will be built with the tritone as a nucleus. One can think of it like a solar system where the tritone is the sun and the other chosen notes are planets.

I will now give a written example of some modal structures which are held together by their relationships through the tritone. One also needn't be irritated if more than one tritone appears in a scale. Only the ordered tritones build this structuring. (see Chapter 4)

- C-Db-E-F#-G-Ab-Bb   This mode belongs to tritone C-F#.
- E-F#-G-A#-B-D-D#   This mode belongs to tritone E-A#.
- Eb-F#-G-A-Bb-C-Db   This mode belongs to tritone Eb-A.
- Bb-Cb-D-E-F-Gb-Ab   This mode belongs to tritone Bb-E.
- Ab-B-C-D-Eb-F-Gb   This mode belongs to tritone Ab-D.
- A-B-C-D#-E-G-G#   This mode belongs to tritone A-D#.

The Scheme in Inversion

- C-Db-E-F#-G-Ab-Bb   This mode belongs to tritone C-F#.
- Ab-Bb-Cb-D-Eb-F#-G   This mode belongs to tritone Ab-D.
- A-B#-C#-D#-E-F#-G   This mode belongs to tritone A-D#.
- D-Eb-F#-G#-A-Bb-C   This mode belongs to tritone D-G#.
- E-G-G#-A#-B-C#-D   This mode belongs to tritone E-A#.
- Eb-F-Gb-A-Bb-C#-D   This mode belongs to tritone Eb-A.

1) HARMONIELEHRE – THEORIE DER MUSTER SYMMETRISCHER ACHSEN

Mein Studium der Harmonik des frühen 20. Jahrhunderts und meine Leidenschaft für den Hard Bop Modern Jazz von 1955 bis heute haben mich angeregt, eine Alternative zu der „Gleichwertigkeit" der Töne zu finden, wie sie in der Dodekaphonie praktiziert wird.

Die Beobachtung von Symmetrieachsen brachte mich auf folgende Tritonus-Reihung: *C-F#, E-A#, Eb-A, B-E, Ab-D, A-D#*. Diese Tritoni bilden den Grundstock der ersten Symmetriereihe. Man kann sie wie bei der Zwölftonreihe umkehren. Das Resultat ist eine weitere Reihe von sechs Tritoni, jedoch in anderer Reihenfolge: *C-F#, Ab-D, A-D#, D-G#, E-A#, Eb-A*.

Nun verteile ich Töne um die Symmetrieachsen, um einen Modus zu bilden und einen Fundus für Melodik und Harmonik zu schaffen. Anders gesagt, ich bilde Modi mit dem Tritonus als Zentrum.

Zur Erläuterung dieses Vorgangs folgen einige Modi, die über den Tritonus aufgebaut sind. Von mehreren Symmetrieachsen in einer Skale sollte man sich nicht verwirren lassen. Nur die Symmetrieachsen, die gezielt geordnet sind, bilden die Struktur (siehe Kapitel 4).

- C-Db-E-F#-G-Ab-B   Dieser Modus gehört zum Tritonus C-F#.
- E-F#-G-A#-H-D-D#   Dieser Modus gehört zum Tritonus E-A#.
- Eb-F#-G-A-B-C-Db   Dieser Modus gehört zum Tritonus Eb-A.
- B-Cb-D-E-F-Gb-Ab   Dieser Modus gehört zum Tritonus B-E.
- Ab-H-C-D-Eb-F-Gb   Dieser Modus gehört zum Tritonus Ab-D.
- A-H-C-D#-E-G-G#   Dieser Modus gehört zum Tritonus A-D#.

Das Schema in Umkehrung:

- C-Db-E-F#-G-Ab-B   Dieser Modus gehört zum Tritonus C-F#.
- Ab-B-Cb-D-Eb-F#-G   Dieser Modus gehört zum Tritonus Ab-D.
- A-H#-C#-D#-E-F#-G   Dieser Modus gehört zum Tritonus A-D#.
- D-Eb-F#-G#-A-B-C   Dieser Modus gehört zum Tritonus D-G#.
- E-G-G#-A#-H-C#-D   Dieser Modus gehört zum Tritonus E-A#.
- Eb-F-Gb-A-B-C#-D   Dieser Modus gehört zum Tritonus Eb-A.

Die Analysen der Musikbeispiele sind im englischen System dargestellt, deswegen erscheint B als Bb und H als B.

EXAMPLE 5

I personally stay with three various modes and their transpositions per piece or movement. This is highly helpful for melodic and harmonic homogeny. For my scheme above I have twelve modes which are all related to each other through the patterning of the tritone. The choice of notes around a given symmetrical axis is personal. If you wish to write mostly darker intervals, fine.

In meinen eigenen Kompositionen verwende ich pro Satz oder Stück nur maximal drei verschiedene Modi. Das bewirkt harmonische und melodische Homogenität.

Dem beschriebenen Schema folgend erhalte ich zwölf Modi, die durch die Stellung der Tritoni miteinander verwandt sind. Die Wahl der Töne um eine Symmetrieachse ist dem persönlichen Geschmack überlassen. Auch dunklere Intervalle sind möglich,

EXAMPLE 6

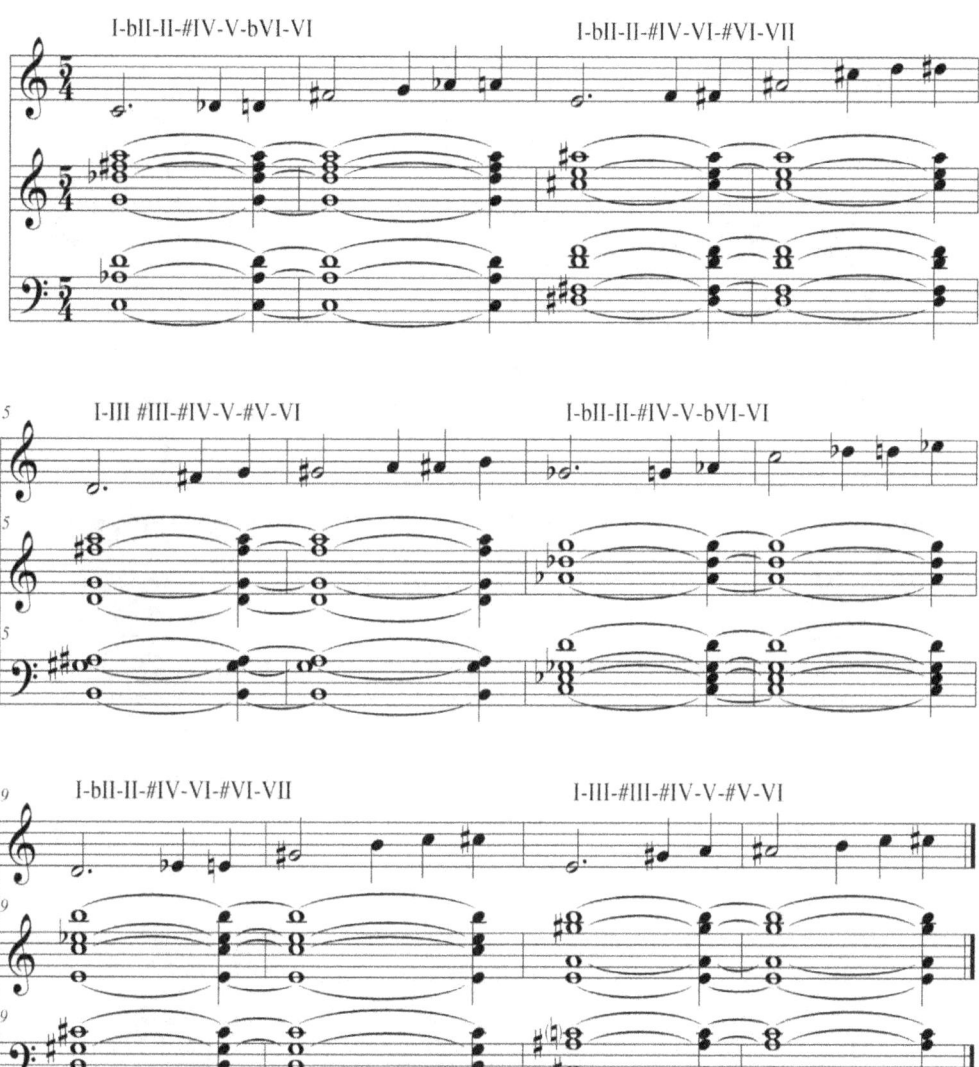

If you wish to write diatonically this of course is also fine.

oder man kann diatonisch arbeiten.

EXAMPLE 7

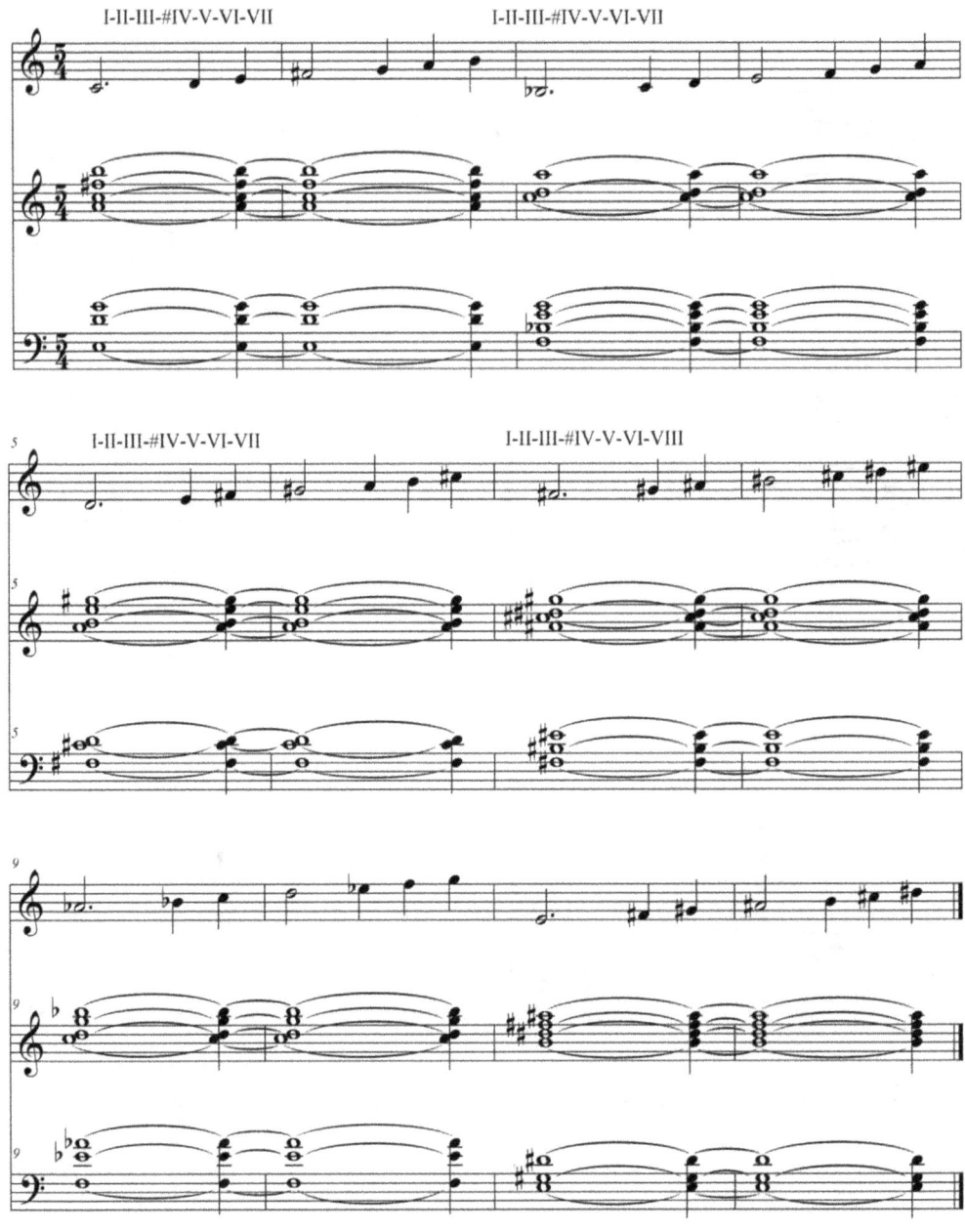

The point of the concept is to move modes with structured symmetrical axes instead of the equality of pitches utilized in dodecaphony. One can build any harmonic palette and arrange the chosen pitches around a given symmetrical axis. When utilizing this method one will hear, as each chosen symmetrical axis moves one to another, a clear and logical harmonic movement.

Der Kerngedanke meines Konzeptes ist, Modi durch strukturierte Symmetrieachsen zu bewegen, anstatt die Gleichstufigkeit der Töne wie in der Dodekaphonie zu verwenden. Man kann die gewünschten Töne frei um eine symmetrische Achse anordnen, und bei jedem Wechsel der Achsen wird eine klare und logische harmonische Bewegung zu hören sein.

EXAMPLE 8

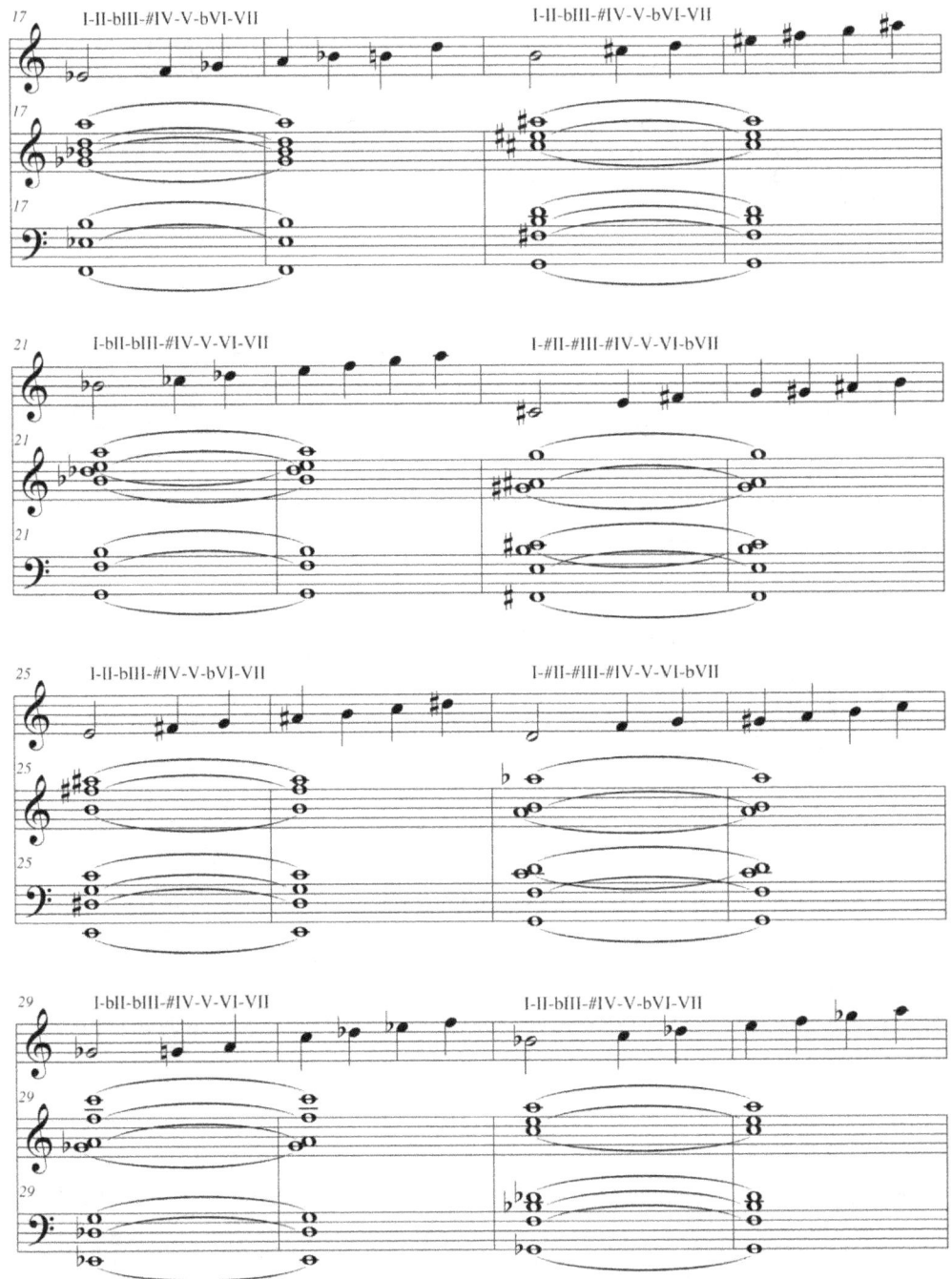

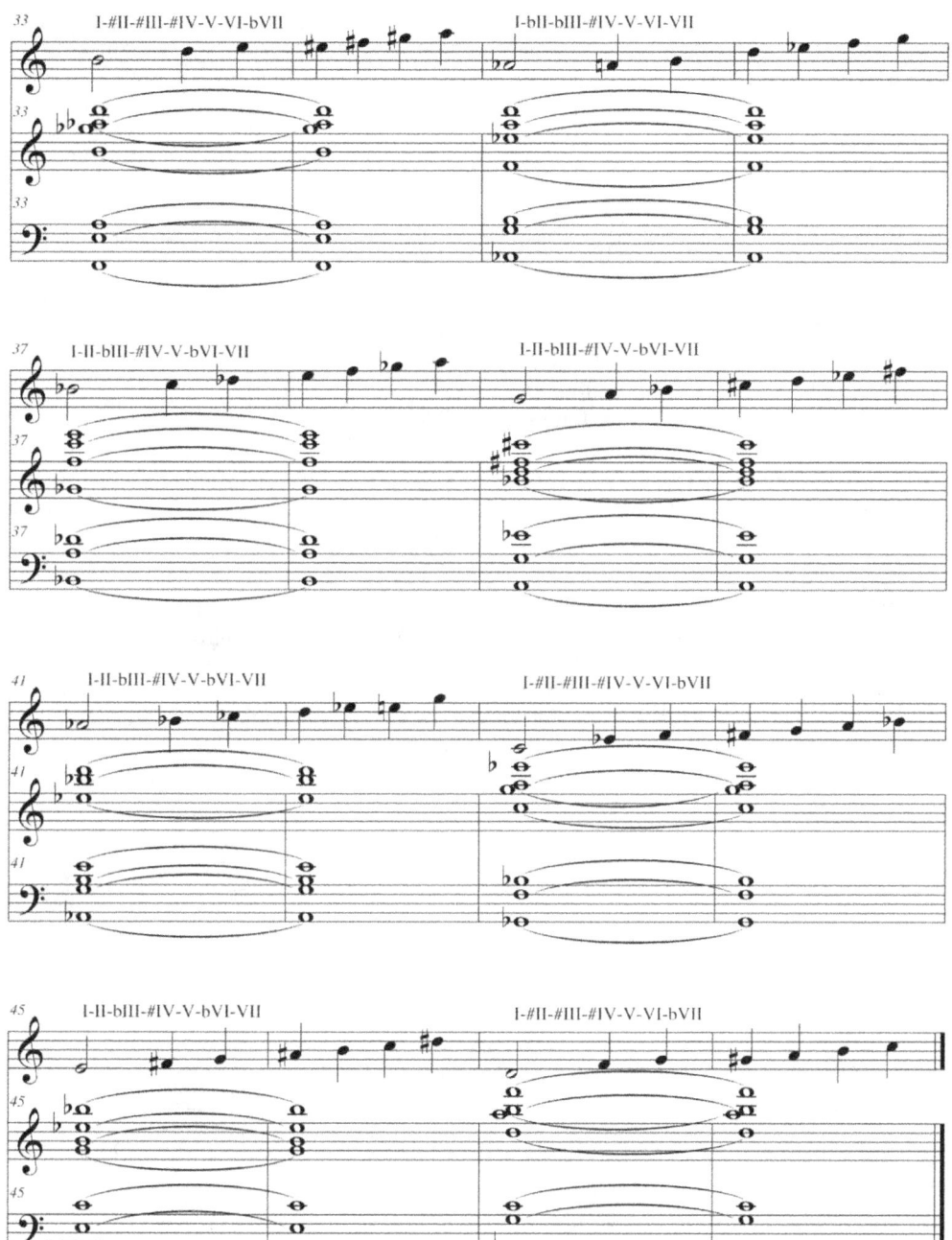

In general, as well, I personally utilize a matrix for my transpositional schematics. This matrix is in itself symmetrical. It looks as such: *I-II-#II-III-#IV-#V-VI-bVII*. This is also not the only possibility for a logical transposition. We can as well develop inverted forms or otherwise related schemes. An example could be *I-bII-III-#II-bVI-V*. In Example 8 the transpositional scheme begins with six modal movements. These present themselves as such *(D-F-E-C-Ab-Bb)*.

(see Example 8 again)

The next row of six modal transpositions is an inverted retrograde of these movements ending on the starting point Db *(F-G-Eb-B-Bb-Db)*. The following six modes are a pure retrograde ending on Ab *(E-D-Gb-Bb-B-Ab)*. And the last six modal movements are a pure inversion of the original starting on Bb *(Bb-G-Ab-C-E-D)*.

The tritone is not the only symmetrical axis in a twelve-note well-tempered environment. We have as well the augmented triad (C-E-G#). This triad can be used to control chromatics exactly in the same manner as I have already shown with the tritone.

EXAMPLE 9

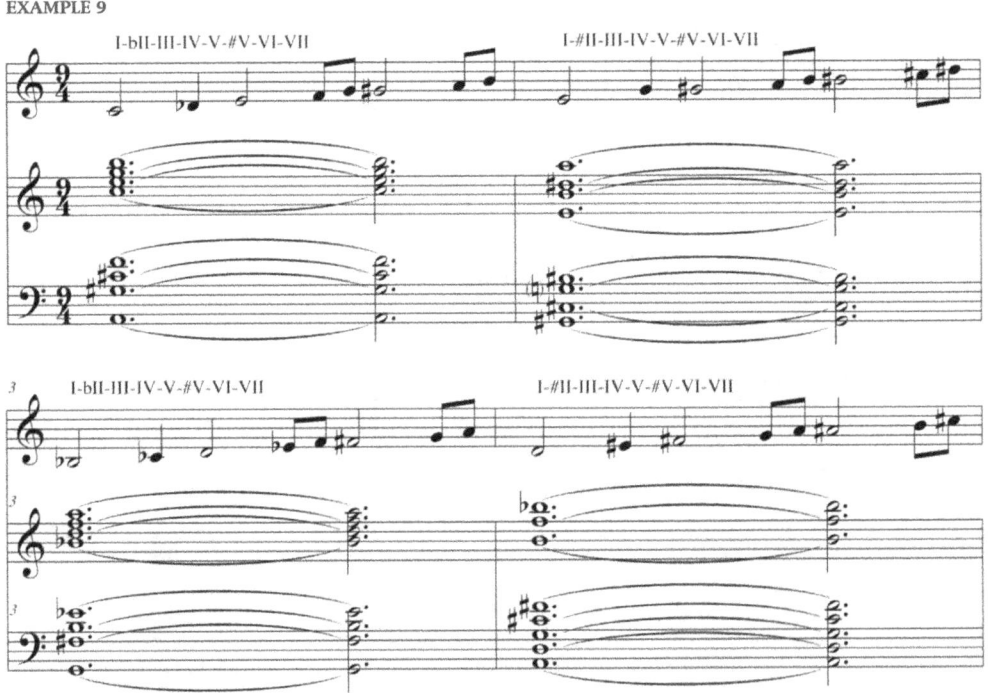

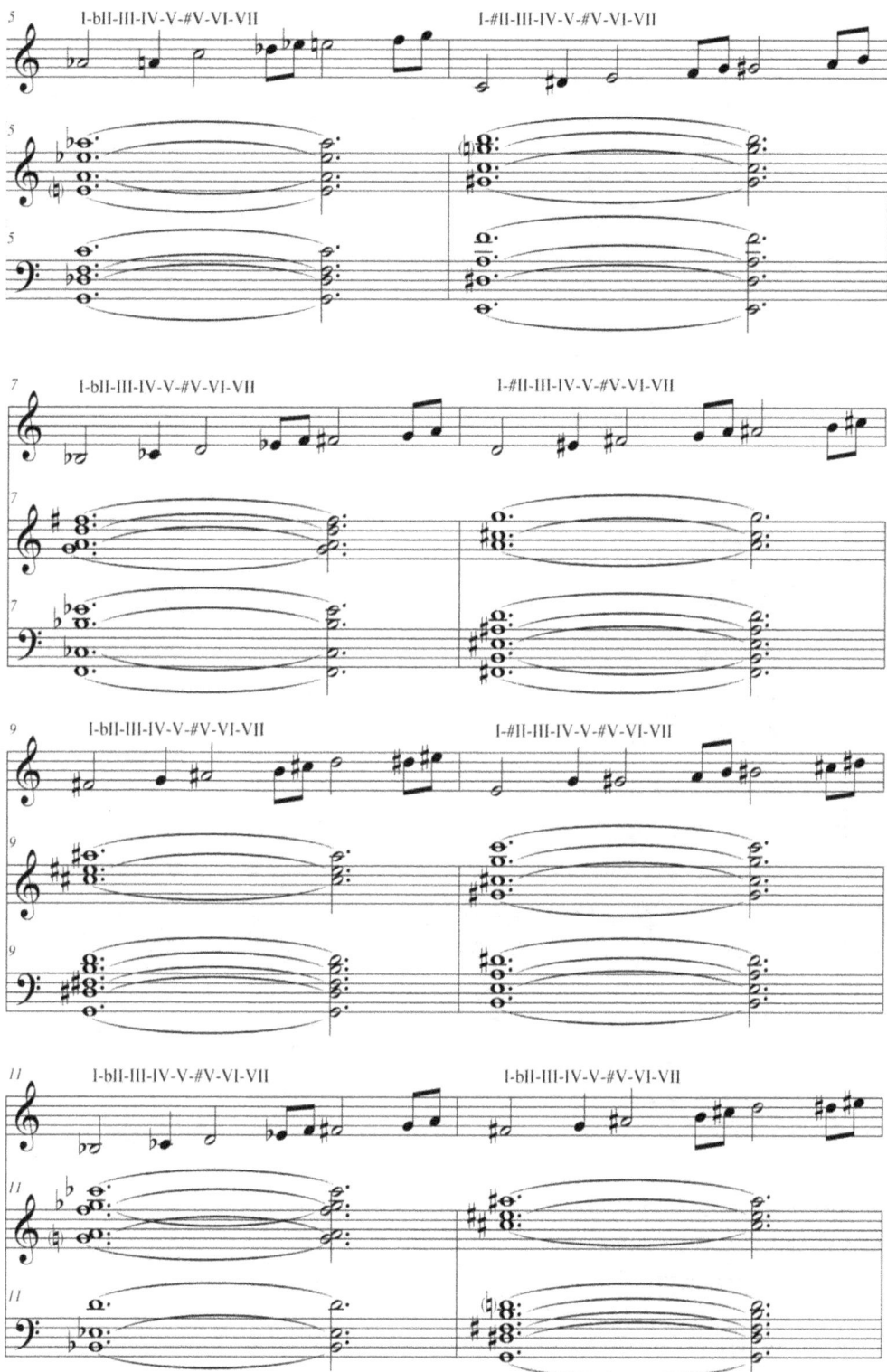

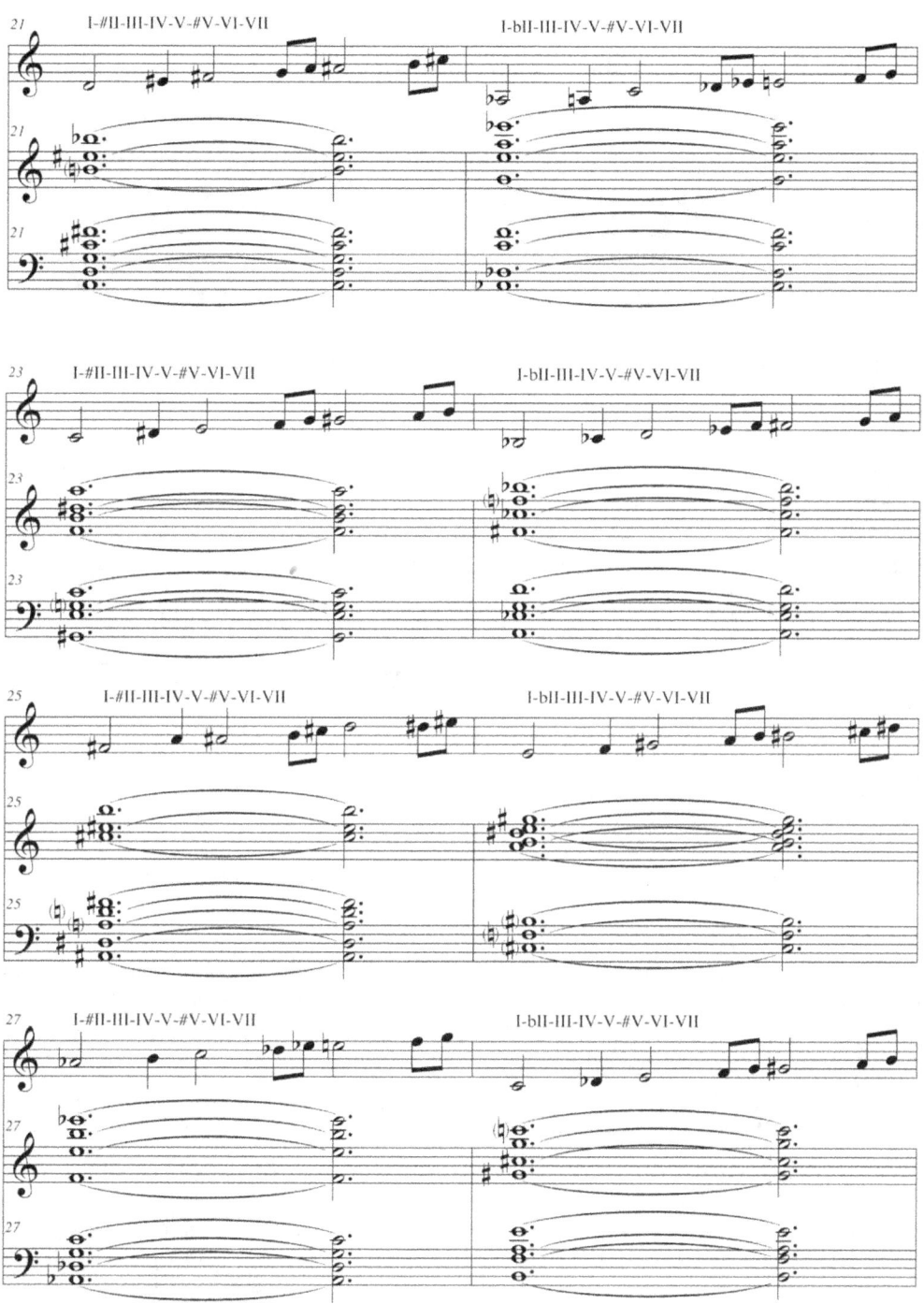

If one wishes to move from a mode with the tritone as the existing center, an augmented fourth or a major third or augmented fifth with the augmented triad as the central symmetry, then one must consider the distribution of notes around the given symmetrical axis. This is in a diatonic example completely clear. From C Lydian to F# Lydian we see that each structure has seven notes. In C we have D and E above C and G, A and B over F#. If we reverse the distribution over C and F# we will hear the harmonic movement of an augmented fourth. In other words then three notes over C and two over F#. (See Chapter 2) Here are various transpositions with a movement the distance of a tritone.

Wenn man einen Modus mit dem Tritonus als Zentrum um eine übermäßige Quarte transponieren möchte – oder im Fall des übermäßigen Dreiklangs um eine Terz oder übermäßige Quinte –, muss man die Verteilung um eine Symmtrischeachse berücksichtigen. In einem diatonischen Beispiel wird dies vollkommen klar. Wir wollen von C lydisch nach Fis lydisch. Beide Strukturen weisen sieben Töne auf. In C lydisch sind D und E über C, und G, A und H über Fis. Wenn wir die Tonverteilung über C und Fis vertauschen, hören wir die harmonische Bewegung einer übermäßigen Quarte. Anders ausgedrückt sind dann drei Töne über C und zwei über Fis (siehe Kapitel 2). Hier sind mehrere Beispiele aufgeführt, die eine harmonische Bewegung eines Tritonus ausführen.

EXAMPLE 10

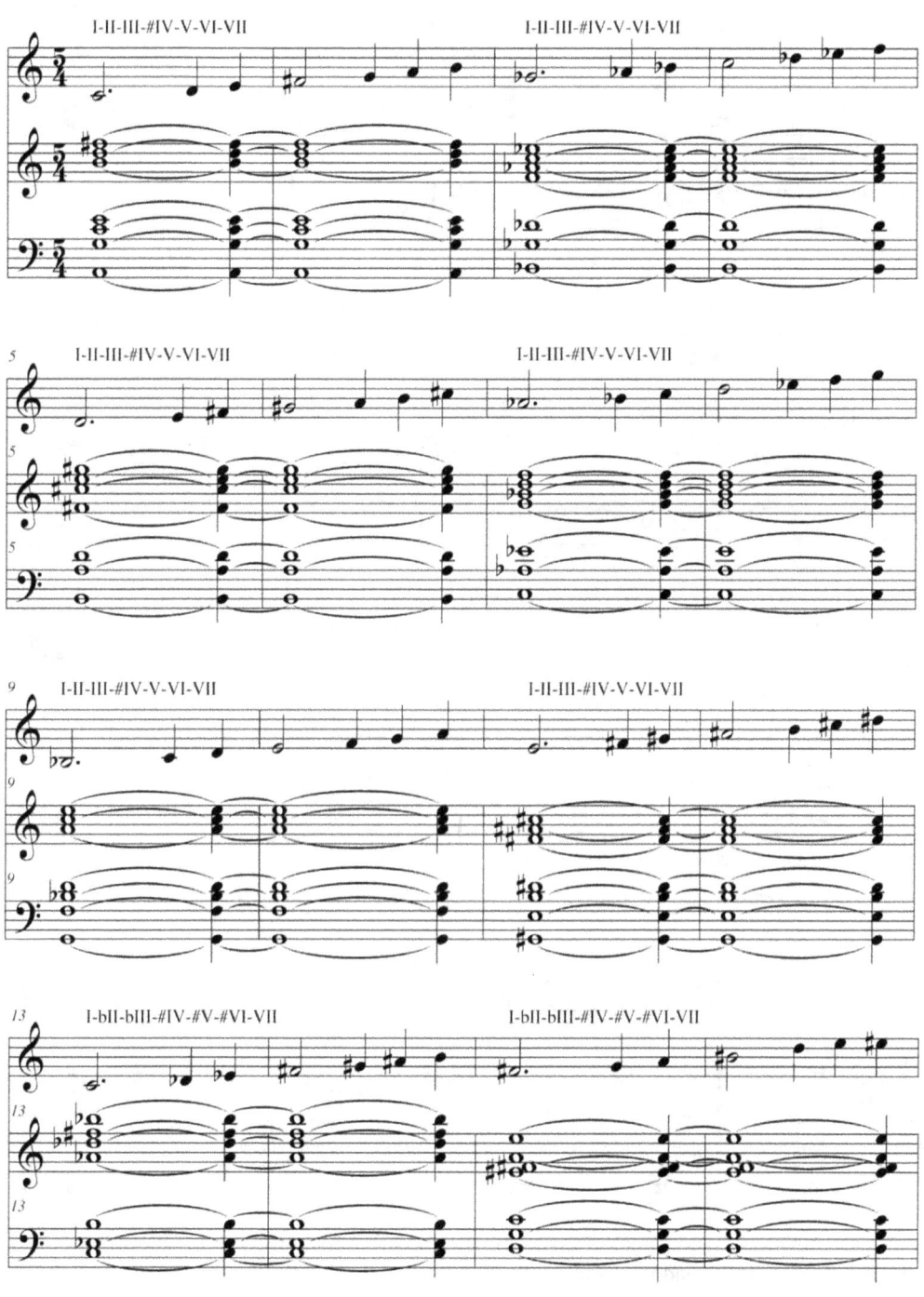

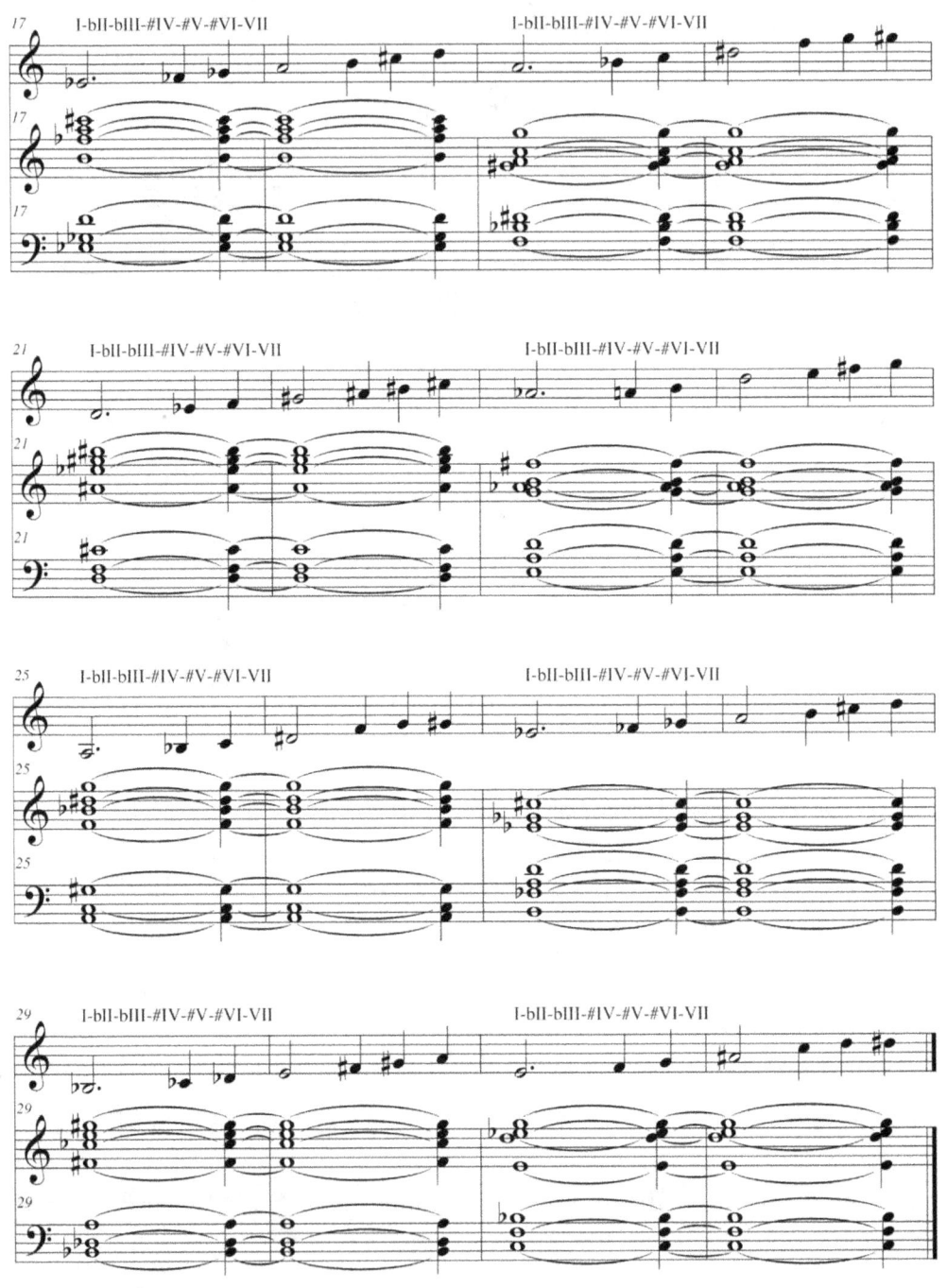

(concerning the augmented triad see Example 9)   (zum übermäßigen Dreiklang siehe Beispiel 9)

2) THE EMERGENCE OF THE STARTING POINT AS A SYMMETRICAL ROOT

A starting point is represented in the thesaurus, (see Chapter 3) with the Roman numeral (I). The term "unequal" represents the method of distributing pitches around a given symmetrical axis. Each mode consists of a prime-numerical symmetrical axis and an unequal distribution of pitches. Here are some examples.

2) DIE ETABLIERUNG EINES GRUNDTONS ALS SYMMETRISCHE WURZEL

Ein Grundton wird in der Modisammlung (siehe Kapitel 3) mit der Ziffer I gekennzeichnet. Der Begriff „ungleich" bezeichnet die Methode, wie Töne um die Achse angeordnet werden. Jeder Modus basiert auf einem Tritonus oder einem übermäßigen Dreiklang und einer ungleichen Verteilung um die Symmetrieachse. Hier einige Beispiele:

EXAMPLE 11

This also enables each mode to be transposed on all half-steps from the original. Here I have a heptatonic mode with the tritone as an axis.

Das macht es, ausgehend vom Original, möglich, jeden Modus auf alle Halbtöne zu transponieren.

EXAMPLE 12

[musical notation: measures 1–12, each labeled I-II-bIII-#IV-V-bVI-VII]

The inequality is either reached through the number of pitches between each part of a given symmetrical axis, as a pure Lydian mode or through an intervallic distance which is greater or smaller. An example of the use of intervallic distance could read as such, I-II-#IV-V.

Die Ungleichheit wird entweder erreicht durch eine unterschiedliche Anzahl an Tönen zwischen den Achsialtönen (z.B. ein rein lydischer Modus), oder durch unterschiedlich große Intervalle. Ein Beispiel für den Gebrauch von unterschiedlichen Intervallabständen wäre I-II-#IV-V.

EXAMPLE 13

In the case of the augmented triad where we have two members of the axis with one pitch above them, the member with two below it will become the starting point.

Im Fall des übermäßigen Dreiklangs, bei dem es zwei Teile der Achse mit einem Ton darüber gibt, bildet die eine Achse mit zwei Tönen darunter den Grundton.

EXAMPLE 14

Also in the case of the augmented triad the distance below also can play a factor. In this particular mode, I-#II-III-IV-#V-VII, the distance above both the (I) and the (#V) are equal however because the intervallic distance is greater beneath (#V) the number (I) becomes the starting point.

Beim übermäßigen Dreiklang kann auch der Intervallabstand unterhalb des Achsialtons eine Rolle spielen. Bei dem Modus I-#II-III-IV-#V-VII ist der Intervallabstand nachfolgend der (I) wie auch nach der (#V) derselbe, aber da der Abstand von der (#V) nach unten größer ist, gilt die (I) als Grundton.

EXAMPLE 15

An interesting acoustical phenomenon occurs if we listen closely to each member of a given mode. I will now build chords of these various modes. Now we shall play each chord firstly and then isolate each separate pitch. We will notice a special dominance of the number (I).
(For a Lydian example see Example 16)

Ein interessantes akustisches Phänomen entsteht, wenn wir jeden Ton eines Modus genau anhören. Um dies zu veranschaulichen, werden wir Akkorde aus verschiedenen Modi bilden. Nun spielen wir jeden einzelnen Akkord zuerst komplett an und danach in Einzeltönen. Wir werden eine signifikante Dominanz der Stufe I hören können. Hier ein lydisches Beispiel:

EXAMPLE 16

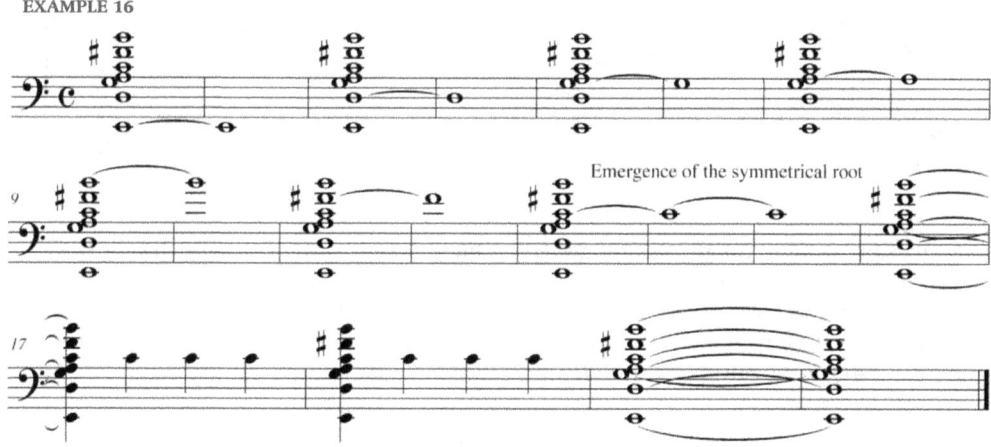

Emergence of the symmetrical root

For a series of Chromatic Lydian modes see Example 17

Hier eine Reihe chromatisch veränderter lydischer Modi:

We can as well examine all of the tritonic modes. We will arbitrarily arrange the notes and place the Roman numeral (I) within a given chord as the second voice. Now I will list all five modal variations in this fashion. V-I-#IV, #V-I-#IV, VI-I-#IV, bVII-#IV, VII-I-#IV.

We will now play each chord firstly and then isolate each separate pitch. The special dominance of the number (I) can also be found in these triads. This dominance I describe as a symmetrical root which can solidify an entire transpositional process.

Im gleichen Sinne können wir alle tritonischen Modi unter die Lupe nehmen. Dafür arrangieren wir spontan die Töne und platzieren die Stufe I in die Mitte eines Akkords. Hier die Liste der fünf modalen Variationen dieser Art: V-I-#IV, #V-I-#IV, VI-I-#IV, bVII-I-#IV, VII-I-#IV.

Wieder spielen wir jeden Akkord als ganzen an und dann in Einzeltönen. Die Dominanz der Stufe I ist auch hier wahrnehmbar. Diese Dominanz sei im Folgenden „symmetrische Wurzel" genannt, sie ebnet dem gesamten Transpositionsprozess den Boden.

EXAMPLE 18

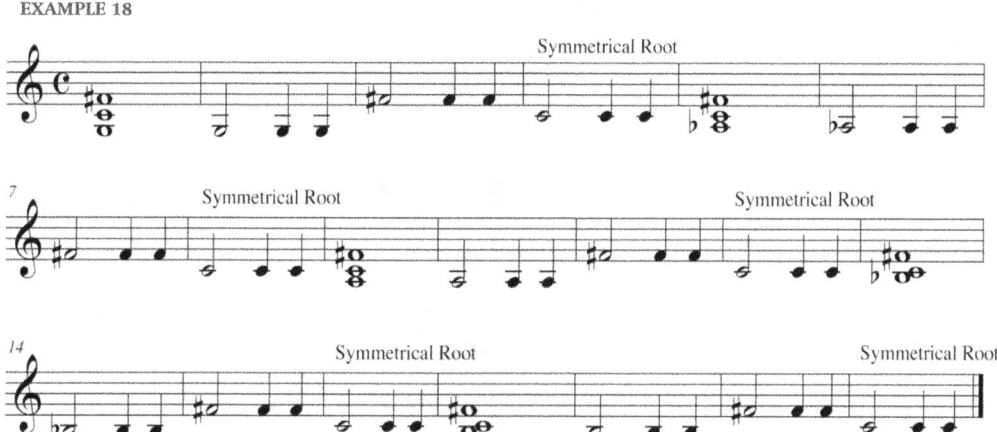

I will now develop a transpositional scheme in which we can follow the appearance of various symmetrical roots. A scheme could be *G-C-F#; Db-Eb-A; Bb-D-G#; A-Bb-E; G-A-D#; E-Ab-D*. Then we will move to F# as our first starting point and invert our scheme. *C#-F#-B#; Db-Eb-A; C-E-A#; G-Ab-D; G-A-D#; Gb-Bb-E*.

Ich werde nun ein Schema zur Transposition entwickeln, in dem wir das Erscheinen verschiedener symmetrischer Wurzeln verfolgen können: *G-C-F#; Db-Eb-A; B-D-G#; A-B-E; G-A-D#; E-Ab-D*. Dann bewegen wir uns zu F# als unserem ersten Ausgangspunkt und kehren unser Schema entsprechend um: *C#-F#-H#; Db-Eb-A; C-E-A#; G-Ab-D; G-A-D#; Gb-B-E*.

EXAMPLE 19

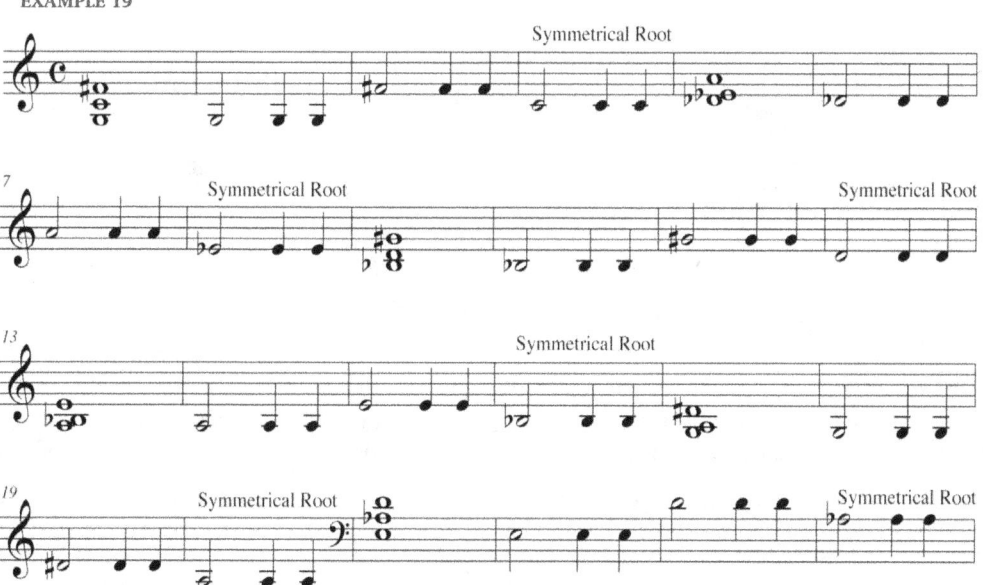

One can hear that in each of our triads the second voice emerges as the symmetrical root.

This principle can therefore be expanded from just three-note modes to encompass all distributions around a particular symmetrical axis possible in our twelve note system. Therefore the generation of quadratonic, pentatonic, hexatonic, heptatonic, octatonic, nonetonic, decatonic, and undecatonic modes.

Es ist hörbar, dass in jedem der Dreiklänge der zweite Ton als symmetrische Wurzel dominiert.

Auf diese Weise kann das Prinzip fortgesetzt werden, von dreitönigen Modi bis hin zu Modi, die alle Töne unseres Zwölftonsystems um die Symmetrieachse verteilt haben. So ergeben sich quadratonische, pentatonische, hexatonische, heptatonische, oktatonische, nonetonische, dekatonische und undekatonische Modi.

EXAMPLE 20

I propose that each mode, because of the exercising of this distributive method, results in the emergence of a symmetrical root as a starting point represented, in this thesaurus, by the Roman numeral (I). (see Thesaurus) The redistribution of modal members through harmonic structures and with the isolation of a given starting point, this pitch always will be audible as possessing dominance even in complex ten or eleven note chords.

Ich behaupte, dass aufgrund des Gebrauchs dieser Verteilungs-Methode bei jedem Modus eine symmetrische Wurzel entsteht (siehe Kapitel 3).

Auch bei einer Verteilung von Noten eines Modus durch harmonische Strukturen (die Isolation eines gegebenen Grundtons vorausgesetzt) wird dieser Ton immer als ein dominantes Element hörbar sein, auch in komplexen Zehn- oder Elf-Ton-Akkorden.

EXAMPLE 21

3) THESAURUS OF TRANPOSABLE UNEQUALLY DISTRIBUTED MODES

As it was presented in the opening of my theory, one can develop modes around a given symmetrical axis as a nucleus. I felt therefore it would be helpful to offer a thesaurus of modalities as a reference for the usage of this technique. One can either harmonically or melodically utilize these modes. For example one can build therewith harmonic sound chambers, as in the music of Scriabin or Roslavec or use the modes horizontally.

TRITONIC MODES
I - #IV - V
I - #IV - #V
I - #IV - VI
I - #IV - bVII
I - #IV - VII

QUADRATONIC MODES
I - II - #IV - V
I - bIII - #IV - V
I - bIII - #IV - #V
I - III - #IV - V
I - III - #IV - #V
I - III - #IV - VI
I - #III - #IV - V
I - #III - #IV - #V
I - #III - #IV - VI
I - #III - #IV - #VI
I - #IV - V - bVI
I - #IV - V - VI
I - #IV - V - bVII
I - #IV - V - VII
I - #IV - #V - VI
I - #IV - #V - bVII
I - #IV - #V - VII
I - #IV - VI - bVII
I - #IV - VI - VII
I - #IV - #VI - VII
I - III - #V - VI
I - III - #V - bVII
I - III - #V - VII

PENTATONIC MODES
I - bII - #IV - V - bVI
I - bII - #IV - V - VI
I - bII - #IV - V - bVII
I - bII - #IV - V - VII
I - bII - #IV - #V - VI
I - bII - #IV - #V - #VI

3) SAMMLUNG TRANSPONIERBARER UNGLEICH VERTEILTER MODI

Wie zu Beginn dargelegt, kann man Modi um eine frei gewählte Symmetrieachse als Mittelpunkt entwickeln. So erschien es mir hilfreich, eine Sammlung als Referenz für den Gebrauch dieser Technik anzubieten. Man kann diese Modi entweder in melodischem oder harmonischem Zusammenhang nutzen, etwa zur Schaffung harmonischer Klangräume wie in der Musik Skrjabins oder Roslawez', oder man gebraucht sie horizontal.

I - bII - #IV - #V - VII
I - bII - #IV - VI - bVII
I - bII - #IV - VI - VII
I - bII - #IV - #VI - VII
I - II - #IV - V - bVI
I - II - #IV - V - VI
I - II - #IV - V - bVII
I - II - #IV - V - VII
I - II - #IV - #V - VI
I - II - #IV - #V - #VII
I - II - #IV - #V - VII
I - II - #IV - VI - bVII
I - II - #IV - VI - VII
I - II - #IV - #VI - VII
I - bIII - #IV - V - bVI
I - bIII - #IV - V - VI
I - bIII - #IV - V - bVII
I - bIII - #IV - V -VII
I - bIII - #IV - #V - VI
I - bIII - #IV - #V - #VI
I - bIII - #IV - #V - VII
I - bIII - #IV - VI - bVII
I - bIII - #IV - VI - VII
I - bIII - #IV - #VI - VII
I - III - #IV - V - bVI
I - III - #IV - V - VI
I - III - #IV - V - bVII
I - III - #IV - V - VII
I - III - #IV - #V - VI
I - III - #IV - #V - #VI
I - III - #IV - #V - VII
I - III - #IV - VI - bVII
I - III - #IV - VI - VII
I - III - #IV - #VI - VII
I - #III - #IV - V - bVI
I - #III - #IV - V - VI
I - #III - #IV - V - bVII
I - #III - #IV - V - VII

I - #III - #IV - #V - VI
I - #III - #IV - #V - #VI
I - #III - #IV - #V - VII
I - #III - #IV - VI - bVII
I - #III - #IV - VI - VII
I - #III - #IV - #VI - VII
I - #IV - V - #V - VI
I - #IV - V - bVI - bVII
I - #IV - V - bVII - VII
I - #IV - V - VI - bVII
I - #IV - V - VI - VII
I - #IV - V - #VI - VII
I - #IV - #V - VI - bVII
I - #IV - #V - VI - VII
I - #IV - #V - #VI - VII
I - #IV - VI - #VI - VII
I - III - #V - VI - bVII
I - III - #V - VI - VII
I - III - #V - #VI - VII
I - III - IV - #V - VI
I - III - IV - #V - bVII
I - III - IV - #V - VII
I - III - V - #V - VI
I - III - V - #V - bVII
I - III - V - #V - VII

HEXATONIC MODES
I - bII - #IV - V - bVI - VI
I - bII - #IV - V - bVI - bVII
I - bII - #IV - V - bVI - VII
I - bII - #IV - V - VI - bVII
I - bII - #IV - V - VI - VII
I - bII - #IV - V - #VI - VII
I - bII - #IV - #V - VI - bVII
I - bII - #IV - #V - VI - VII
I - bII - #IV - #V - #VI - VII
I - bII - #IV - VI - #VI - VII
I - II - #IV - V - bVI - VI
I - II - #IV - V - bVI - bVII
I - II - #IV - V - bVI - VII
I - II - #IV - V - VI - bVII
I - II - #IV - V - VI - VII
I - II - #IV - V - #VI - VII
I - II - #IV - #V - VI - bVII
I - II - #IV - #V - VI - VII
I - II - #IV - #V - #VI - VII
I - II - #IV - VI - #VI - VII
I - bIII - #IV - V - bVI - VI
I - bIII - #IV - V - bVI - bVII
I - bIII - #IV - V - bVI - VII
I - bIII - #IV - V - VI - bVII
I - bIII - #IV - V - VI - VII
I - bIII - #IV - V - #VI - VII
I - bIII - #IV - #V - VI - bVII

I - bIII - #IV - #V - VI - VII
I - bIII - #IV - #V - #VI - VII
I - bIII - #IV - VI - #VI - VII
I - III - #IV - V - bVI - VI
I - III - #IV - V - bVI - bVII
I - III - #IV - V - bVI - VII
I - III - #IV - V - VI - bVII
I - III - #IV - V - VI - VII
I - III - #IV - V - #VI - VII
I - III - #IV - #V - VI - bVII
I - III - #IV - #V - VI - VII
I - III - #IV - #V - #VI - VII
I - III - #IV - VI - #VI - VII
I - #III - #IV - V - bVI - VI
I - #III - #IV - V - bVI - bVII
I - #III - #IV - V - bVI - VII
I - #III - #IV - V - VI - bVII
I - #III - #IV - V - VI - VII
I - #III - #IV - V - #VI - VII
I - #III - #IV - #V - VI - bVII
I - #III - #IV - #V - VI - VII
I - #III - #IV - #V - #VI - VII
I - #III - #IV - VI - #VI - VII
I - bII - bIII - #IV - V - bVI
I - bII - III - #IV - V - bVI
I - bII - III - #IV - V - VI
I - bII - #III - #IV - V - bVI
I - bII - #III - #IV - V - VI
I - bII - #III - #IV - V - bVII
I - II - bIII - #IV - V - bVI
I - II - bIII - #IV - V - VI
I - II - bIII - #IV - V - bVII
I - II - bIII - #IV - V - VII
I - II - III - #IV - V - bVI
I - II - III - #IV - V - VI
I - II - III - #IV - V - bVII
I - II - III - #IV - V - VII
I - II - III - #IV - #V - VI
I - II - #III - #IV - V - bVI
I - II - #III - #IV - V - VI
I - II - #III - #IV - V - bVII
I - II - #III - #IV - V - VII
I - II - #III - #IV - #V - VI
I - II - #III - #IV - #V - bVII
I - #II - III - #IV - V - bVI
I - #II - III - #IV - V - VI
I - #II - III - #IV - V - bVII
I - #II - III - #IV - V - VII
I - #II - III - #IV - #V - VI
I - #II - III - #IV - #V - bVII

(Prometheiischer Klangkörper)

I - #II - III - #IV - #V - VII
I - #II - #III - #IV - V - bVI
I - #II - #III - #IV - V - VI
I - #II - #III - #IV - V - bVII
I - #II - #III - #IV - V - VII
I - #II - #III - #IV - #V - VI
I - #II - #III - #IV - #V - bVII
I - #II - #III - #IV - #V - VII
I - #II - #III - #IV - VI - bVII
I - III - #III - #IV - V - bVI
I - III - #III - #IV - V - VI
I - III - #III - #IV - V - bVII
I - III - #III - #IV - V - VII
I - III - #III - #IV - #V - VI
I - III - #III - #IV - #V - bVII
I - III - #III - #IV - #V - VII
I - III - #III - #IV - VI - bVII
I - III - #III - #IV - VI - VII
I - #IV - V - #V - VI - bVII
I - #IV - V - #V - VI - VII
I - #IV - V - bVI - #VI - VII
I - #IV - V - VI - #VI - VII
I - #IV - #V - VI - #VI - VII
I - III - #V - VI - #VI - VII
I - III - IV - V - #V - VI
I - III - IV - V - #V - #VI
I - III - IV - V - #V - VII
I - III - IV - #V - VI - bVII
I - III - IV - #V - VI - VII
I - III - IV - #V - #VI - VII
I - III - V - #V - VI - bVII
I - III - V - #V - VI - VII
I - III - V - #V - #VI - VII
I - II - III - IV - #V - VI
I - II - III - IV - #V - bVII
I - #II - III - IV - #V - VI
I - #II - III - IV - #V - bVII
I - #II - III - IV - #V - VII

HEPTATONIC MODES
I - bII - #IV - V - bVI - VI - bVII
I - bII - #IV - V - bVI - VI - VII
I - bII - #IV - V - bVI - #VI - VII
I - bII - #IV - V - VI - bVII - VII
I - bII - #IV - #V - VI - bVII - VII
I - II - #IV - V - bVI - VI - bVII
I - II - #IV - V - bVI - VI - VII
I - II - #IV - V - bVI - bVII - VII
I - II - #IV - V - VI - bVII - VII
I - II - #IV - #V - VI - bVII - VII
I - bIII - #IV - V - bVI - VI - bVII

I - bIII - #IV - V - bVI - VI - VII
I - bIII - #IV - V - bVI - bVII - VII
I - bIII - #IV - V - VI - bVII - VII
I - bIII - #IV - #V - VI - bVII - VII
I - III - #IV - V - bVI - VI - bVII
I - III - #IV - V - bVI - VI - VII
I - III - #IV - V - bVI - bVII - VII
I - III - #IV - V - VI - bVII - VII
I - III - #IV - #V - VI - bVII - VII
I - #III - #IV - V - bVI - VI - bVII
I - #III - #IV - V - bVI - VI - VII
I - #III - #IV - V - bVI - bVII - VII
I - #III - #IV - V - VI - bVII - VII
I - #III - #IV - #V - VI - bVII - VII
I - #IV - V - #V - VI - #VI - VII
I - bII - II - #IV - V - #V - VI
I - bII - II - #IV - V - bVI - bVII
I - bII - II - #IV - V - bVI - VII
I - bII - II - #IV - V - VI - bVII
I - bII - II - #IV - V - VI - VII
I - bII - II - #IV - V - #VI - VII
I - bII - II - #IV - #V - VI - bVII
I - bII - II - #IV - #V - VI - VII
I - bII - II - #IV - #V - #VI - VII
I - bII - II - #IV - VI - #VI - VII
I - bII - bIII - #IV - V - #V - VI
I - bII - bIII - #IV - V - bVI - bVII
I - bII - bIII - #IV - V - bVI - VII
I - bII - bIII - #IV - V - VI - bVII
I - bII - bIII - #IV - V - VI - VII
I - bII - bIII - #IV - V - #VI - VII
I - bII - bIII - #IV - #V - VI - bVII
I - bII - bIII - #IV - #V - VI - VII
I - bII - bIII - #IV - #V - #VI - VII
I - bII - bIII - #IV - VI - #VI - VII
I - bII - III - #IV - V - #V - VI
I - bII - III - #IV - V - bVI - bVII
I - bII - III - #IV - V - bVI - VII
I - bII - III - #IV - V - VI - bVII
I - bII - III - #IV - V - VI - VII
I - bII - III - #IV - V - #VI - VII
I - bII - III - #IV - #V - VI - bVII
I - bII - III - #IV - #V - VI - VII
I - bII - III - #IV - #V - #VI - VII
I - bII - III - #IV - VI - #VI - VII
I - bII - #III - #IV - V - #V - VI
I - bII - #III - #IV - V - bVI - bVII
I - bII - #III - #IV - V - bVI - VII
I - bII - #III - #IV - V - VI - bVII
I - bII - #III - #IV - V - VI - VII
I - bII - #III - #IV - V - #VI - VII
I - bII - #III - #IV - #V - VI - bVII
I - bII - #III - #IV - #V - VI - VII
I - bII - #III - #IV - #V - #VI - VII

I - bII - #III - #IV - VI - #VI - VII
I - II - bIII - #IV - V - #V - VI
I - II - bIII - #IV - V - bVI - bVII
I - II - bIII - #IV - V - bVI - VII
I - II - bIII - #IV - V - VI - bVII
I - II - bIII - #IV - V - VI - VII
I - II - bIII - #IV - V - #VI - VII
I - II - bIII - #IV - #V - VI - bVII
I - II - bIII - #IV - #V - VI - VII
I - II - bIII - #IV - #V - #VI - VII
I - II - bIII - #IV - VI - #VI - VII
I - II - III - #IV - V - #V - VI
I - II - III - #IV - V - bVI - bVII
I - II - III - #IV - V - bVI - VII
I - II - III - #IV - V - VI - bVII
I - II - III - #IV - V - VI - VII
I - II - III - #IV - V - #VI - VII
I - II - III - #IV - #V - VI - bVII
I - II - III - #IV - #V - VI - VII
I - II - III - #IV - #V - #VI - VII
I - II - III - #IV - VI - #VI - VII
I - II - #III - #IV - V - #V - VI
I - II - #III - #IV - V - bVI - bVII
I - II - #III - #IV - V - bVI - VII
I - II - #III - #IV - V - VI - bVII
I - II - #III - #IV - V - VI - VII
I - II - #III - #IV - V - #VI - VII
I - II - #III - #IV - #V - VI - bVII
I - II - #III - #IV - #V - VI - VII
I - II - #III - #IV - #V - #VI - VII
I - II - #III - #IV - VI - #VI - VII
I - #II - III - #IV - V - #V - VI
I - #II - III - #IV - V - bVI - bVII
I - #II - III - #IV - V - bVI - VII
I - #II - III - #IV - V - VI - bVII
I - #II - III - #IV - V - VI - VII
I - #II - III - #IV - V - #VI - VII
I - #II - III - #IV - #V - VI - bVII
I - #II - III - #IV - #V - VI - VII
I - #II - III - #IV - #V - #VI - VII
I - #II - III - #IV - VI - #VI - VII
I - #II - #III - #IV - V - #V - VI
I - #II - #III - #IV - V - bVI - bVII
I - #II - #III - #IV - V - bVI - VII
I - #II - #III - #IV - V - VI - bVII
I - #II - #III - #IV - V - VI - VII
I - #II - #III - #IV - V - #VI - VII
I - #II - #III - #IV - #V - VI - bVII
I - #II - #III - #IV - #V - VI - VII
I - #II - #III - #IV - #V - #VI - VII
I - #II - #III - #IV - VI - #VI - VII
I - III - #III - #IV - V - #V - VI
I - III - #III - #IV - V - bVI - bVII
I - III - #III - #IV - V - bVI - VII

I - III - #III - #IV - V - VI - bVII
I - III - #III - #IV - V - VI - VII
I - III - #III - #IV - V - #VI - VII
I - III - #III - #IV - #V - VI - bVII
I - III - #III - #IV - #V - VI - VII
I - III - #III - #IV - #V - #VI - VII
I - III - #III - #IV - VI - #VI - VII
I - III - IV - #V - VI - #VI - VII
I - III - V - #V - VI - #VI - VII
I - III - IV - V - #V - VI - bVII
I - III - IV - V - #V - VI - VII
I - III - IV - V - #V - #VI - VII
I - bII - III - IV - #V - VI - bVII
I - bII - III - IV - #V - VI - VII
I - bII - III - IV - #V - #VI - VII
I - bII - III - V - #V - VI - bVII
I - bII - III - V - #V - VI - VII
I - bII - III - V - #V - #VI - VII
I - II - III - IV - #V - VI - bVII
I - II - III - IV - #V - VI - VII
I - II - III - IV - #V - #VI - VII
I - II - III - V - #V - VI - bVII
I - II - III - V - #V - VI - VII
I - II - III - V - #V - #VI - VII
I - #II - III - IV - #V - VI - bVII
I - #II - III - IV - #V - VI - VII
I - #II - III - IV - #V - #VI - VII
I - #II - III - V - #V - VI - bVII
I - #II - III - V - #V - VI - VII
I - #II - III - V - #V - #VI - VII

OCTATONIC MODES
I - bII - #IV - V - bVI - VI - bVII - VII
I - II - #IV - V - bVI - VI - bVII - VII
I - bIII - #IV - V - bVI - VI - bVII - VII
I - III - #IV - V - bVI - VI - bVII - VII
I - #III - #IV - V - bVI - VI - bVII - VII
I - bII - II - #IV - V - bVI - VI - bVII
I - bII - II - #IV - V - bVI - VI - VII
I - bII - II - #IV - V - bVI - #VI - VII
I - bII - II - #IV - V - VI - #VI - VII
I - bII - II - #IV - #V - VI - bVII - VII
I - bII - bIII - #IV - V - bVI - VI - bVII
I - bII - bIII - #IV - V - bVI - VI - VII
I - bII - bIII - #IV - V - bVI - #VI - VII
I - bII - bIII - #IV - V - VI - #VI - VII
I - bII - bIII - #IV - #V - VI - bVII - VII
I - bII - III - #IV - V - bVI - VI - bVII
I - bII - III - #IV - V - bVI - VI - VII
I - bII - III - #IV - V - bVI - #VI - VII
I - bII - III - #IV - V - VI - #VI - VII

I - bII - III - #IV - #V - VI - bVII - VII
I - bII - #III - #IV - V - bVI - VI - bVII
I - bII - #III - #IV - V - bVI - VI - VII
I - bII - #III - #IV - V - bVI - #VI - VII
I - bII - #III - #IV - V - VI - #VI - VII
I - bII - #III - #IV - #V - VI - bVII - VII
I - II - bIII - #IV - V - bVI - VI - bVII
I - II - bIII - #IV - V - bVI - VI - VII
I - II - bIII - #IV - V - bVI - #VI - VII
I - II - bIII - #IV - V - VI - #VI - VII
I - II - bIII - #IV - #V - VI - bVII - VII
I - II - III - #IV - V - bVI - VI - bVII
I - II - III - #IV - V - bVI - VI - VII
I - II - III - #IV - V - bVI - #VI - VII
I - II - III - #IV - V - VI - #VI - VII
I - II - III - #IV - #V - VI - bVII - VII
I - II - #III - #IV - V - bVI - VI - bVII
I - II - #III - #IV - V - bVI - VI - VII
I - II - #III - #IV - V - bVI - #VI - VII
I - II - #III - #IV - V - VI - #VI - VII
I - II - #III - #IV - #V - VI - bVII - VII
I - #II - III - #IV - V - bVI - VI - bVII
I - #II - III - #IV - V - bVI - VI - VII
I - #II - III - #IV - V - bVI - #VI - VII
I - #II - III - #IV - V - VI - #VI - VII
I - #II - III - #IV - #V - VI - bVII - VII
I - #II - #III - #IV - V - bVI - VI - bVII
I - #II - #III - #IV - V - bVI - VI - VII
I - #II - #III - #IV - V -bVI - #VI - VII
I - #II - #III - #IV - V - VI - #VI - VII
I - #II - #III - #IV - #V - VI - bVII - VII
I - III - #III - #IV - V - bVI - VI - bVII
I - III - #III - #IV - V - bVI - VI - VII
I - III - #III - #IV - V - bVI - #VI - VII
I - III - #III - #IV - V - VI - #VI - VII
I - III - #III - #IV - #V - VI - bVII - VII
I - bII - II - III - #IV - V - #V - VI
I - bII - II - #III - #IV - V - #V - VI
I - bII - II - #III - #IV - V -bVI - bVII
I - bII - #II - III - #IV - V - #V - VI
I - bII - #II - III - #IV - V - bVI - bVII
I - bII - #II - III - #IV -V - bVI - VII
I - bII - #II - #III - #IV - V - #V - VI
I - bII - #II - #III - #IV - V -bVI - bVII
I - bII - #II - #III - #IV - V - bVI - VII
I - bII - #II - #III - #IV - V - VI - bVII
I - bII - III - #III - #IV -V - #V - VI
I - bII - III - #III - #IV - V - bVI - bVII
I - bII - III - #III - #IV - V - bVI - VII
I - bII - III - #III - #IV - V - VI - bVII
I - bII - III - #III - #IV - V - VI - VII
I - II - #II - III - #IV - V - #V - VI
I - II - #II - III - #IV - V - bVI - bVII
I - II - #II - III - #IV - V - bVI - VII

I - II - #II - III - #IV - V - VI - bVII
I - II - #II - III - #IV - V - VI - VII
I - II - #II - III - #IV - V - #VI - VII
I - II - #II - #III - #IV - V - #V - VI
I - II - #II - #III - #IV - V - bVI - bVII
I - II - #II - #III - #IV - V - bVI - VII
I - II - #II - #III - #IV - V - VI - bVII
I - II - #II - #III - #IV - V - VI - VII
I - II - #II - #III - #IV - V - #VI - VII
I - II - #II - #III - #IV - #V - VI - bVII
I - II - III - #III - #IV - V - #V - VI
I - II - III - #III - #IV - V - bVI - bVII
I - II - III - #III - #IV - V - bVI - VII
I - II - III - #III - #IV - V - VI - bVII
I - II - III - #III - #IV - V - VI - VII
I - II - III - #III - #IV - V - #VI - VII
I - II - III - #III - #IV - #V - VI - bVII
I - II - III - #III - #IV - #V - VI - VII
I - #II - III - #III - #IV - V - #V - VI
I - #II - III - #III - #IV - V - bVI - bVII
I - #II - III - #III - #IV - V - bVI - VII
I - #II - III - #III - #IV - V - VI - bVII
I - #II - III - #III - #IV - V - VI - VII
I - #II - III - #III - #IV - V - #VI - VII
I - #II - III - #III - #IV - #V - VI - bVII
I - #II - III - #III - #IV - #V - VI - VII
I - #II - III - #III - #IV - #V - #VI - VII
I - III - IV - V - #V - VI - #VI - VII
I - bII - III - IV - V - #V - VI - bVII
I - bII - III - IV - V - #V - VI - VII
I - bII - III - IV - V - #V - #VI - VII
I - II - III - IV - V - #V - VI - bVII
I - II - III - IV - V - #V - VI - VII
I - II - III - IV - V - #V - #VI - VII
I - #II - III - IV - V - #V - VI - bVII
I - #II - III - IV - V - #V - VI - VII
I - #II - III - IV - V - #V - #VI - VII

NONETONIC MODES
I - bII - II - #IV - V - bVI - VI - bVII - VII
I - bII - bIII - #IV - V - bVI - VI - bVII - VII
I - bII - III - #IV - V - bVI - VI - bVII - VII
I - bII - #III - #IV - V - bVI - VI - bVII - VII
I - II - bIII - #IV - V - bVI - VI - bVII - VII
I - II - III - #IV - V - bVI - VI - bVII - VII
I - II - #III - #IV - V - bVI - VI - bVII - VII
I - #II - III - #IV - V - bVI - VI - bVII - VII
I - #II - #III - #IV - V - bVI - VI - bVII - VII
I - III - #III - #IV - V - bVI - VI - bVII - VII
I - bII - II - bIII - #IV - V - bVI - VI - bVII
I - bII - II - bIII - #IV - V - bVI - VI - VII
I - bII - II - bIII- #IV - V - bVI - #VI - VII
I - bII - II - bIII- #IV - V - VI - #VI - VII

I - bII - II - bIII - #IV - #V - VI - bVII - VII
I - bII - II - III - #IV - V - bVI - VI - bVII
I - bII - II - III - #IV - V - bVI - VI - VII
I - bII - II - III - #IV - V - bVI - #VI - VII
I - bII - II - III - #IV - V - VI - #VI - VII
I - bII - II - III - #IV - #V - VI - bVII - VII
I - bII - II - #III - #IV - V - bVI - VI - bVII
I - bII - II - #III - #IV - V - bVI - VI - VII
I - bII - II - #III - #IV - V - bVI - #VI - VII
I - bII - II - #III - #IV - V - VI - #VI - VII
I - bII - II - #III - #IV - #V - VI - bVII - VII
I - II - #II - III - #IV - V - bVI - VI - bVII
I - II - #II - III - #IV - V - bVI - VI - VII
I - II - #II - III - #IV - V - bVI - #VI - VII
I - II - #II - III - #IV - V - VI - #VI - VII
I - II - #II - III - #IV - #V - VI - bVII - VII
I - II - #II - #III - #IV - V - bVI - VI - bVII
I - II - #II - #III - #IV - V - bVI - VI - VII
I - II - #II - #III - #IV - V - bVI - #VI - VII
I - II - #II - #III - #IV - V - VI - #VI - VII
I - II - #II - #III - #IV - #V - VI - bVII - VII
I - II - III - #III - #IV - V - bVI - VI - bVII
I - II - III - #III - #IV - V - bVI - VI - VII
I - II - III - #III - #IV - V - bVI - #VI - VII
I - II - III - #III - #IV - V - VI - #VI - VII
I - II - III - #III - #IV - #V - VI - bVII - VII
I - #II - III - #III - #IV - V - bVI - VI - bVII
I - #II - III - #III - #IV - V - bVI - VI - VII
I - #II - III - #III - #IV - V - bVI - #VI - VII
I - #II - III - #III - #IV - V - VI - #VI - VII
I - #II - III - #III - #IV - #V - VI - bVII - VII
I - bII - III - IV - V - #V - VI - #VI - VII
I - II - III - IV - V - #V - VI - #VI - VII
I - #II - III - IV - V - #V - VI - #VI - VII
I - II - #II - III - IV - V - #V - VI - VII
I - II - #II - III - IV - V - #V - #VI - VII

DECATONIC MODES
I - bII - II - bIII - #IV - V - bVI - VI - bVII - VII
I - bII - II - III - #IV - V - bVI - VI - bVII - VII
I - bII - II - #III - #IV - V - bVI - VI - bVII - VII
I - bII - #II - III - #IV - V - bVI - VI - bVII - VII
I - bII - #II - #III - #IV - V - bVI - VI - bVII - VII
I - bII - III - #III - #IV - V - bVI - VI - bVII - VII
I - II - #II - III - #IV - V - bVI - VI - bVII - VII
I - II - #II - #III - #IV - V - bVI - VI - bVII - VII
I - II - III - #III - #IV - V - bVI - VI - bVII - VII
I - #II - III - #III - #IV - V - bVI - VI - bVII - VII
I - bII - II - #II - #III - #IV - V - bVI - VI - bVII
I - bII - II - III - #III - #IV - V - bVI - VI - bVII
I - bII - II - III - #III - #IV - V - bVI - VI - VII
I - bII - #II - III - #III - #IV - V - bVI - VI - bVII
I - bII - #II - III - #III - #IV - V - bVI - VI - VII
I - bII - #II - III - #III - #IV - V - bVI - #VI - VII

I - II - #II - III - #III - #IV - V - bVI - VI - bVII
I - II - #II - III - #III - #IV - V - bVI - VI - VII
I - II - #II - III - #III - #IV - V - bVI - #VI - VII
I - II - #II - III - #III - #IV - V - VI - #VI - VII
I - bII - II - III - IV - V - #V - VI - #VI - VII
I - bII - #II - III - IV - V - #V - VI - #VI - VII
I - II - #II - III - IV - V - #V - VI - #VI - VII

UNDECATONIC MODES
I - bII - II - bIII - III - #IV - V - bVI - VI - bVII - VII
I - bII - II - bIII - #III - #IV - V - bVI - VI - bVII - VII
I - bII - II - III - #III - #IV - V - bVI - VI - bVII - VII
I - bII - #II - III - #III - #IV - V -bVI - VI - bVII - VII
I - II - #II - III - #III - #IV - V - bVI - VI - bVII - VII

PARTIALLY TRANSPOSABLE SYMMETRIC MODES

QUADRATONIC MODES
I - bII - #IV - V
I - II - #IV - #V
I - III - #IV - bVII
I - #III - #IV - VII

HEXATONIC MODES
I - bII - II - #IV - V - #V
I - bII - #II - #IV - V - VI
I - bII - III - #IV - V - bVII
I - II - bIII - #IV - #V - VI
I - II - #III - #IV - #V - VII
I - #II - III - #IV - VI - bVII
I - #II - #III - #IV - VI - VII
I - III - #III - #IV - #VI - VII
I - bII - III - IV - #V - IV
I - #II - III - V - #V - VII

OCTATONIC MODES
I - bII - II - bIII - #IV - V - #V - VI
I - bII - II - III - #IV - V - #V - bVII
I - bII - II - #III - #IV - V - #V - VII
I - bII - #II - III - #IV - V - VI - bVII
I - bII - III - #III - #IV - V - bVII - VII
I - II - #II - III - #IV - #V - VI - bVII
I - II - bIII - #III - #IV - #V - VI - VII
I - II - III - #III - #IV - #V - #VI - VII
I - #II - III - #III - #IV - VI - #VI - VII

NONETONIC MODES
I - bII - II - III - IV - #IV - #V - VI - bVII
I - bII - #II - III - IV - V - #V - VI - VII
I - II - #II - III - #III - #IV - V - #V - #VI - VII

DECATONIC MODES
I - bII - II - bIII - III - #IV - V - #V - VI - bVII
I - bII - II - bIII - #III - #IV - V - #V - VI - VII
I - II - #II - III - #III - #IV - #V - VI - #VI - VII

Finally is also possible to integrate the above mentioned "partially transposable symmetric modes" as a tool for building harmonic movement. By employing the principle of the "greater intervallic distance" we can receive the effect of a "symmetrical root" with an entire symmetrical axis.

Taking the example *I-II-bIII-#IV-#V-VI* we see the symmetrical axis Eb-A has an entire minor third above it before another symmetrical axis appears. Therefore this axis rings stronger through the entire structure. We can therefore utilize the entire symmetrical axis as a transpositional starting point. I will now build a logical chord progression using symmetrical axes instead of symmetrical roots.

Schließlich ist es möglich, die letzte Reihe von teilweise transponierbaren symmetrischen Modi als Werkzeug zu verwenden, um harmonische Bewegungen zu erreichen. Mit dem Prinzip der größeren Intervallabstände wird eine komplette symmetrische Achse zu einer Art symmetrischer Wurzel.

Nehmen wir ein Beispiel *I-II-bIII-#IV-#V-VI*. Wir sehen, dass die symmetrische Achse Eb-A eine gesamte kleine Terz über sich hat, bevor eine weitere Achse erscheint. Dafür klingt diese Achse stärker als die anderen zwei. Deswegen können wir diese Achse als Ausgangspunkt für ein Transpositionsschema nutzen. Ich werde jetzt mit der Verwendung symmetrischer Achsen statt symmetrischer Wurzeln eine logische Akkordfolge aufbauen.

EXAMPLE 21a

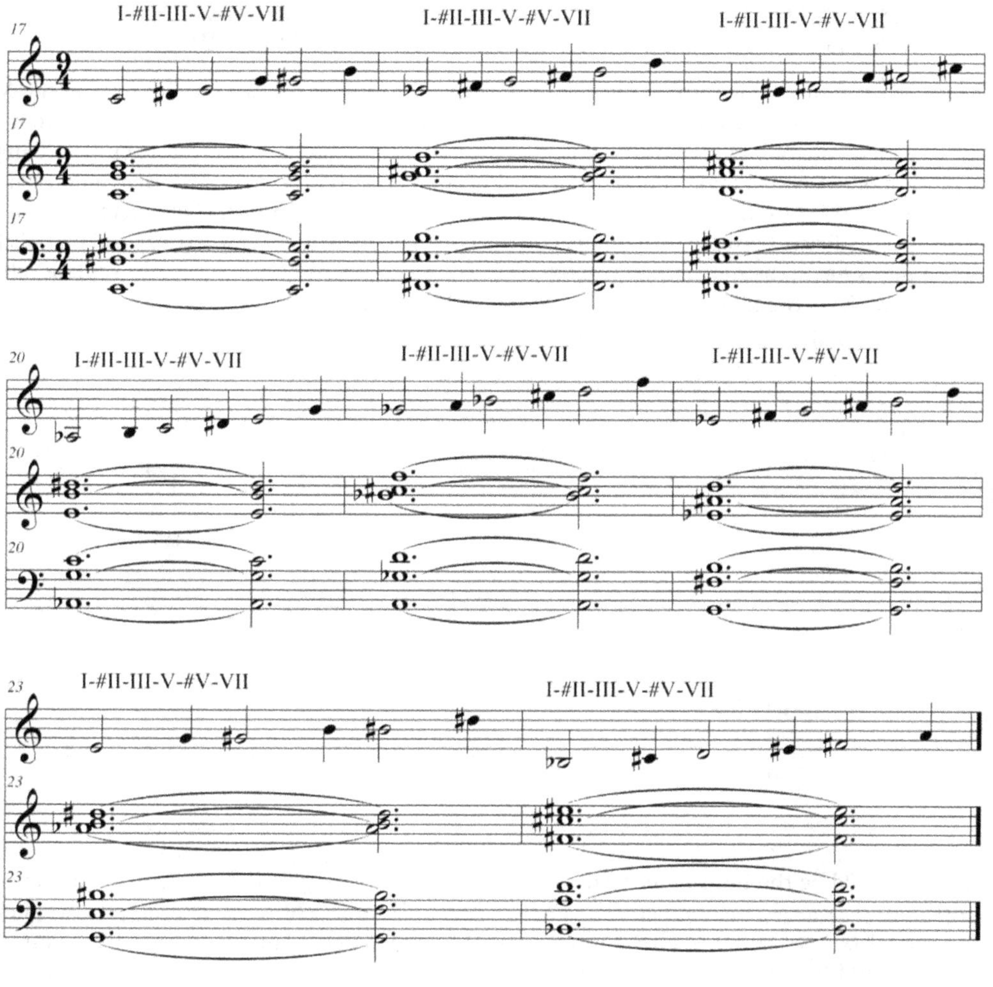

With some "partially transposable symmetric modes" the intervallic distance over two axis can be identical. Then the shorter distance "below" a given axis determines the starting point.

Bei manchen teilweise transponierbaren symmetrischen Modi ist der Intervallabstand zweier symmetrischer Achsen gleich. In diesem Falle ist die symmetrische Achse mit dem kleinsten Intervallabstand unter sich der Ausgangspunkt.

EXAMPLE 21b

4) THE APPLICATIONS OF MODES WITH MULTIPLE SYMMETRIES

As we can decipher many modes which are non-diatonic have in many instances multiple tritones or perhaps as well an augmented triad which co-exist in a given mode. One example could be the formula *I-bII-III-#IV-V-VI-bVII*. This mode has a total of three tritones found between its members. The first of course is *I-#IV*, the next is between bII and V and lastly we have the tritone *bVII-III*.

4) DIE ANWENDUNG VON MODI MIT MEHREREN SYMMETRIEACHSEN

In vielen Fällen besitzen nicht-diatonische Modi neben den Symmetrieachsen mehrere Tritoni oder vielleicht auch einen übermäßigen Dreiklang. In dem Modus *I-bII-III-#IV-V-VI-bVII* finden wir beispielsweise drei Tritoni. Der erste Tritonus ist natürlich *I-#IV* (die Symmetrieachse), der nächste besteht zwischen bII und V und schließlich der dritte von *bVII* nach *III*.

EXAMPLE 22

One application could be the limiting of transpositional possibilities resulting in no repetition of a given symmetrical axis. An example with this particular method could be *C-Db-E-F#-G-A-Bb<>Ab-A-C-D-Eb-F-Gb<>Eb-E-G-A-Bb-C-Db<>G-Ab-B-C#-D-E-F-<>Db-D-F-G-Ab-Bb-Cb<>A-Bb-C#-D#-E-F#-G<>D-Eb-F#-G#-A-B-C.*

Eine Anwendung könnte die Begrenzung der Transpositionsmöglichkeiten sein, womit wir keinen folgenden Modus mit einer derselben Symmetrieachsen haben.

Ein Beispiel für diese besondere Technik:

C-Db-E-F#-G-A-B<>Ab-A-C-D-Eb-F-Gb<>Eb-Fb-G-A-B-C-Db<>G-Ab-H-C#-D-E-F-<>Db-D-F-G-Ab-B-Cb<>A-B-C#-D#-E-F#-G<>D-Eb-F#-G#-A-H-C.

EXAMPLE 23

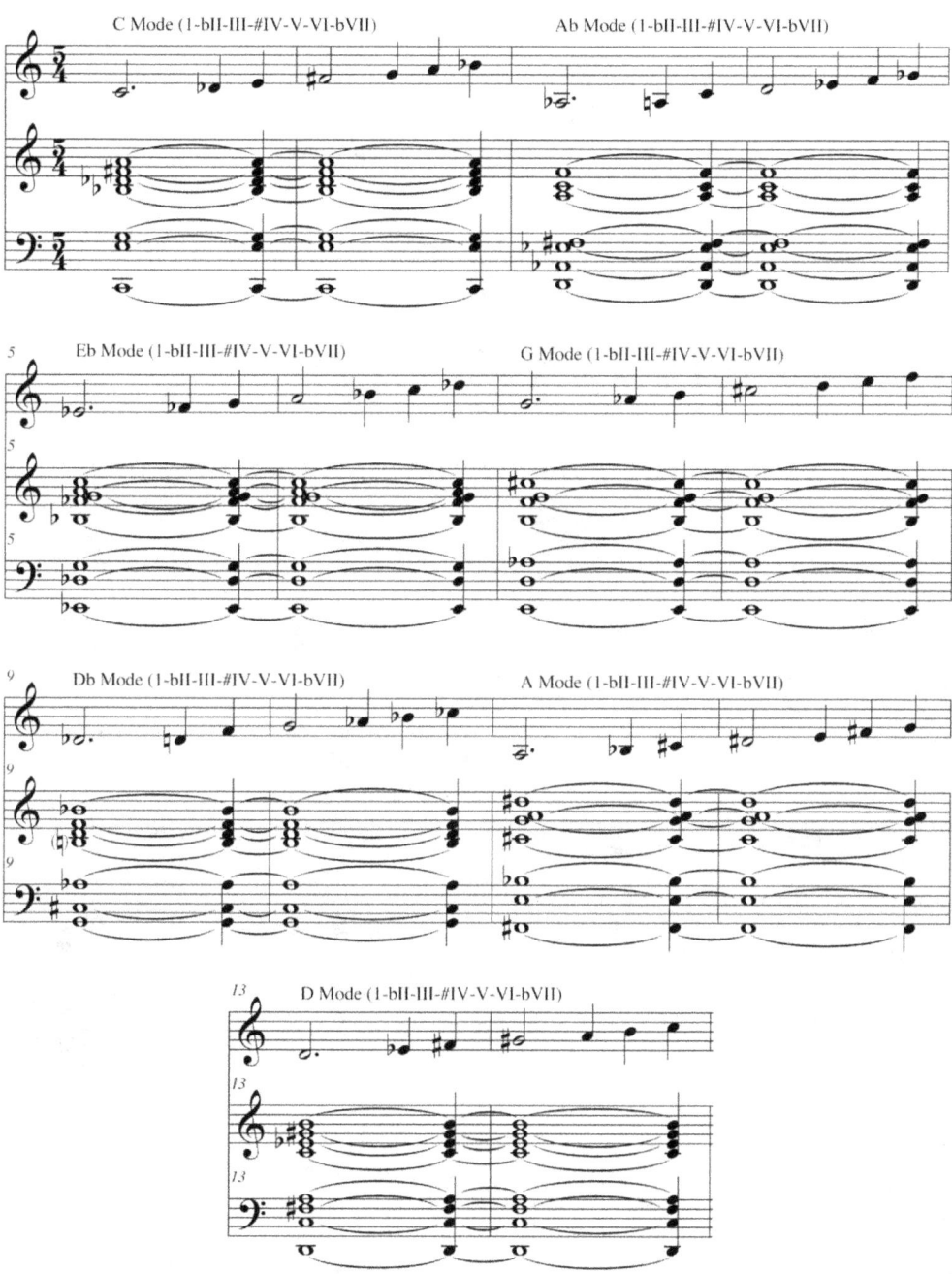

Here we will invert the transpositions giving us another row without repetition. I will begin this time with F# as our first starting point.

Ab hier werden wir die Transpositionen umkehren, was eine weitere Reihe Modi ohne Wiederholungen erbringt. Der Ausgangspunkt wird dieses Mal das F# sein:

40

F#-G-A#-H#-C#-D#-E <> Bb-Cb-D-E-F-G-Ab <> Eb-Fb-G-A-B-C-Db <> B-C-D#-E#-F#-G#-A <> F-Gb-A-H-C-D-Eb <> A-B-C#-D#-E-F#-G <> E-F-G#-A#-H-C#-D <>.

F#-G-A#-H#-C#-D#-E <> B-Cb-D-E-F-G-Ab <> Eb-Fb-G-A-B-C-Db <> H-C-D#-E#-F#-G#-A <> F-Gb-A-H-C-D-Eb <> A-B-C#-D#-E-F#-G <> E-F-G#-A#-H-C#-D <>.

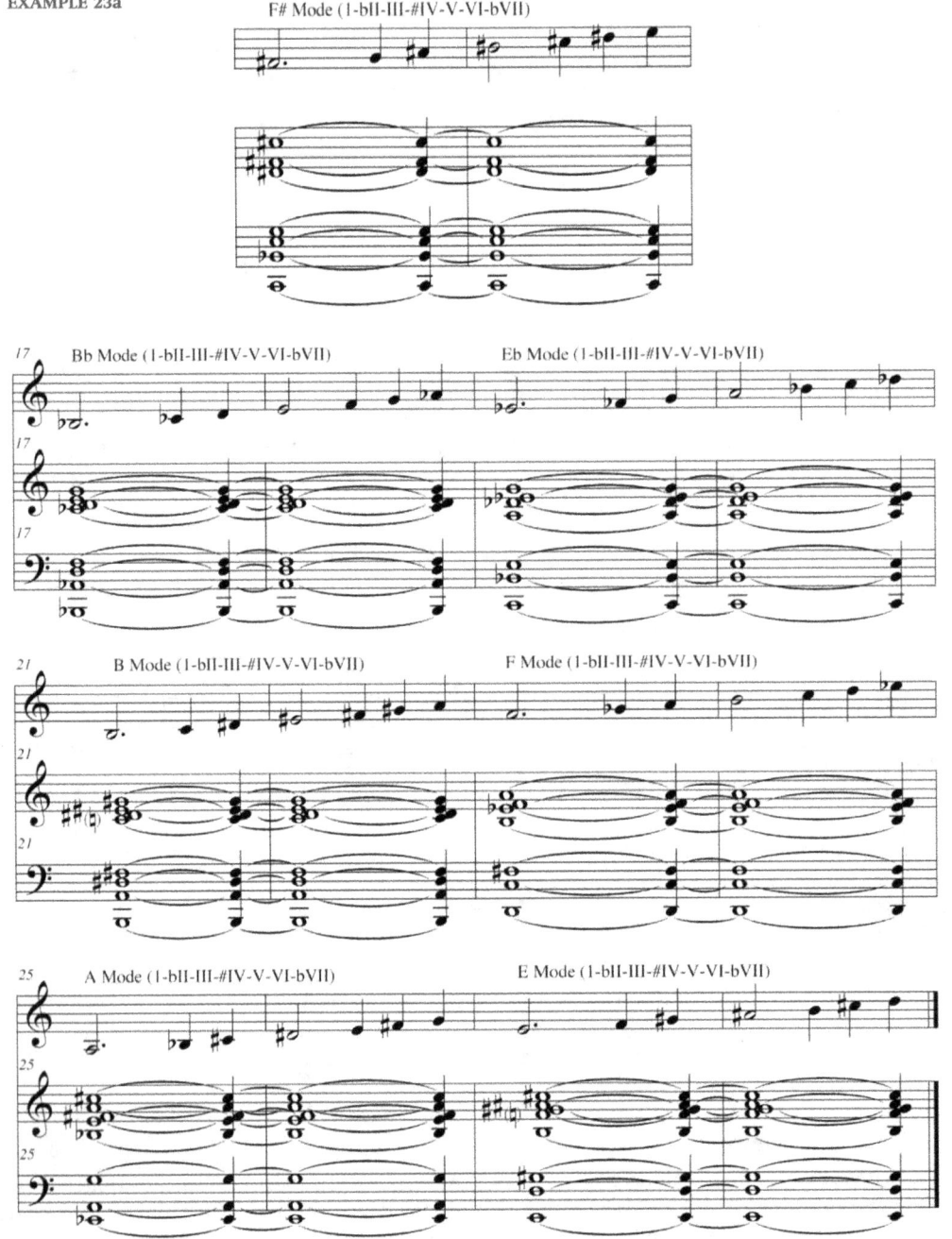

EXAMPLE 23a

I will now derive all three unequally distributed modes from the original and begin these modes all with C. "Mode 1" will remain C-Db-E-F#-G-A-Bb "Mode 2" begins from Db however from C it appears as such C-D#-E#-F#-G#-A-B. "Mode 3" begins on Bb and it shows itself as C-D-Eb-F#-G#-A-B.

Nun wollen wir alle drei ungleich verteilten Modi vom Ursprungsmodus herleiten. Alle drei sollen auf „C" beginnen. „Modus 1" bleibt C-Db-E-F#-G-A-B, „Modus 2" beginnt auf Db, doch von C aus erscheint er C-D#-E#-F#-G#-A-H, „Modus 3" beginnt auf B, von C ausgehend C-D-Eb-F#-G#-A-H.

EXAMPLE 24

Now we will use all three variants as starting points. Each mode of course is constructed with the tritone as the nucleus and varying planets. This gives us the possibility of various transpositional schemes without always using simply the original mode.

An exposition of this technique shows that each mode in the thesaurus, although some may have the same intervallic construction can be utilized to create an alternative logical schematic.

This is what I mean when I say only the tritones which are ordered bring about this structuring. (See Chapter 1)

I will now present a scheme with all three modal variants. We will see that the transpositional scheme is solid and that "Mode 1" can be found in each mode however "Mode 1" will in total not in any way form a logical set of transpositions. It is only with the usage of "Mode 2" and "Mode 3" that the logic comes to be. Here is an example. C-Db-E-F#-G-A-Bb (mode 1) E-F#-G-A#-B#-C#-D# (mode 3) D-F-G-G#-A#-B-C# (mode 2) Bb-Cb-D-E-F-G-Ab (mode 1) Ab-B-C#-D-E-F-G (mode 2) Db-Eb-Fb-G-A-Bb-C (mode 3).

Alle drei Variationen sollen nun als eine symmetrische Wurzel verwendet werden. Jeder der Modi ist natürlich aus dem Tritonus als Kern und unterschiedlichen Tönen konstruiert. Dies eröffnet uns die Möglichkeit verschiedener Transpositionsschemata, ohne jedes Mal „nur" den Original-Modus zu verwenden. Eine Darlegung dieser Technik zeigt, dass jeder Modus in der Sammlung aus Kapitel 3 dazu benutzt werden kann, ein alternatives logisches Schema zu erzeugen, obwohl einige Modi vielleicht dieselbe Intervallkonstruktion besitzen. Dieser Vorgang beweist deutlich die Richtigkeit der Aussage, dass nur die geordnete Symmetrieachse diese Struktur hervorbringt (siehe Kapitel 1).

Nun vereinen wir alle drei modalen Variationen in einem Schema. Es wird sich zeigen, dass das Transpositionsschema stabil ist. "Modus 1" findet sich in jedem weiteren Modus wieder, obwohl derselbe in keiner Weise eine logische Abfolge von Transpositionen formen wird. Nur durch die Verwendung von „Modus 2" und „Modus 3" entsteht ein logischer Ablauf: C-Db-E-F#-G-A-B (Modus 1) E-F#-G-A#-H#-C#-D# (Modus 3) D-F-G-G#-A#-H-C# (Modus 2) B-Cb-D-E-F-G-Ab (Modus 1) Ab-H-C#-D-E-F-G (Modus 2) Db-Eb-Fb-G-A-B-C (Modus 3).

42

EXAMPLE 25

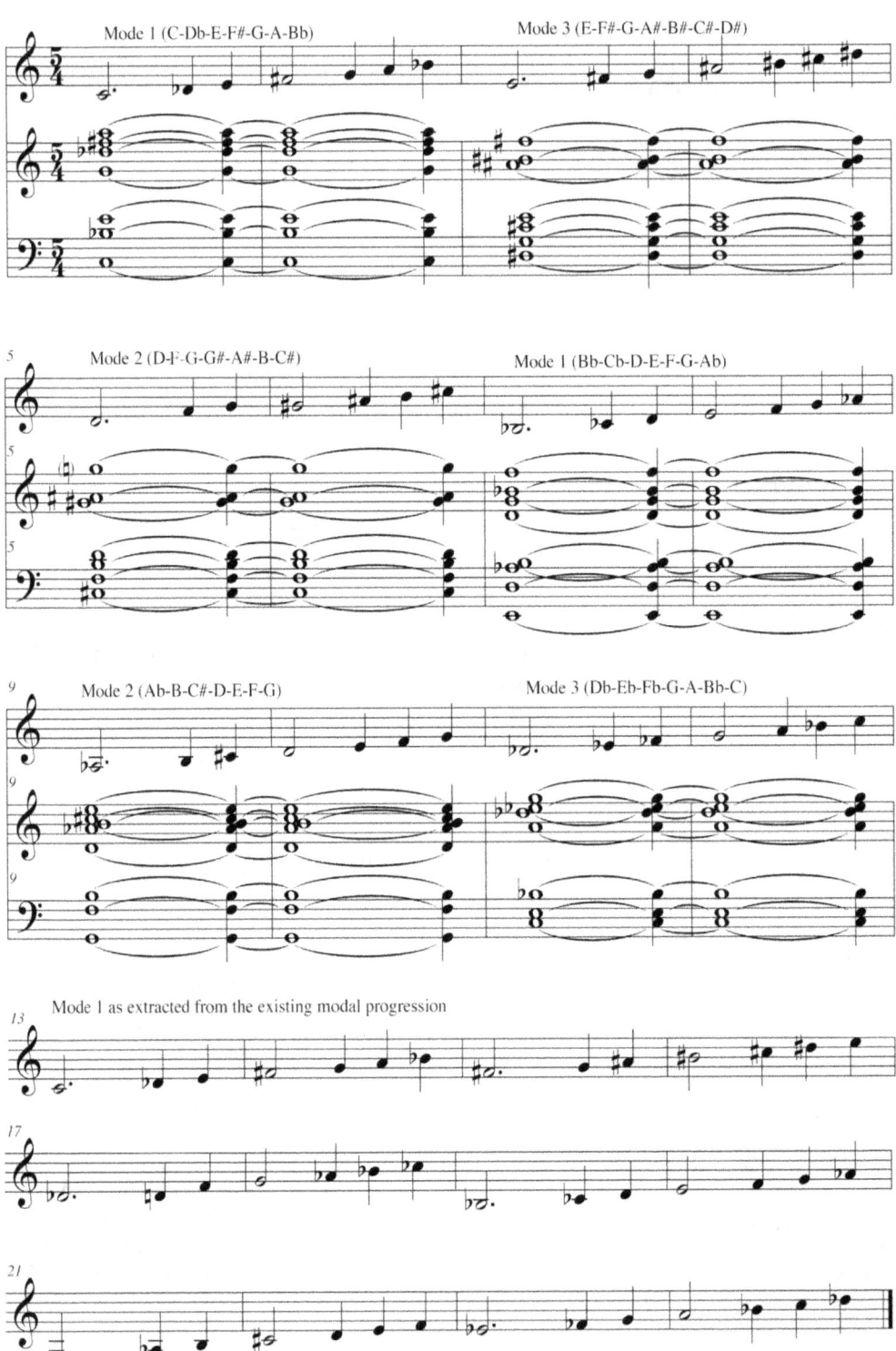

The above is my first part of the scheme, now I will invert the transpositions from *F#*. Once again "Mode 1" will not be the binding force. *F#-G-A#-B#-C#-D#-E* (mode 1) *D-E-F-G#-A#-B-C#* (mode 3) *E-G-A-A#-B-C#-D#* (mode 2) *Ab-A-C-D-Eb-F-Gb* (mode 1) *Bb-C#-D#-E-F#-G-A* (mode 2) *F-G-Ab-B-C#-D-E* (mode 3).

Dies ist der erste Teil des Schemas, jetzt kehren wir die Transpositionen auf *F#* um. Wieder wird „Modus 1" nicht der formgebende sein: *F#-G-A#-H#-C#-D#-E* (Modus1) *D-E-F-G#-A#-H-C#* (Modus 3) *E-G-A-A#-H-C#-D#* (Modus 2) *Ab-A-C-D-Eb-F-Gb* (Modus 1) *B-C#-D#-E-F#-G-A* (Modus 2) *F-G-Ab-H-C#-D-E* (Modus 3).

EXAMPLE 26

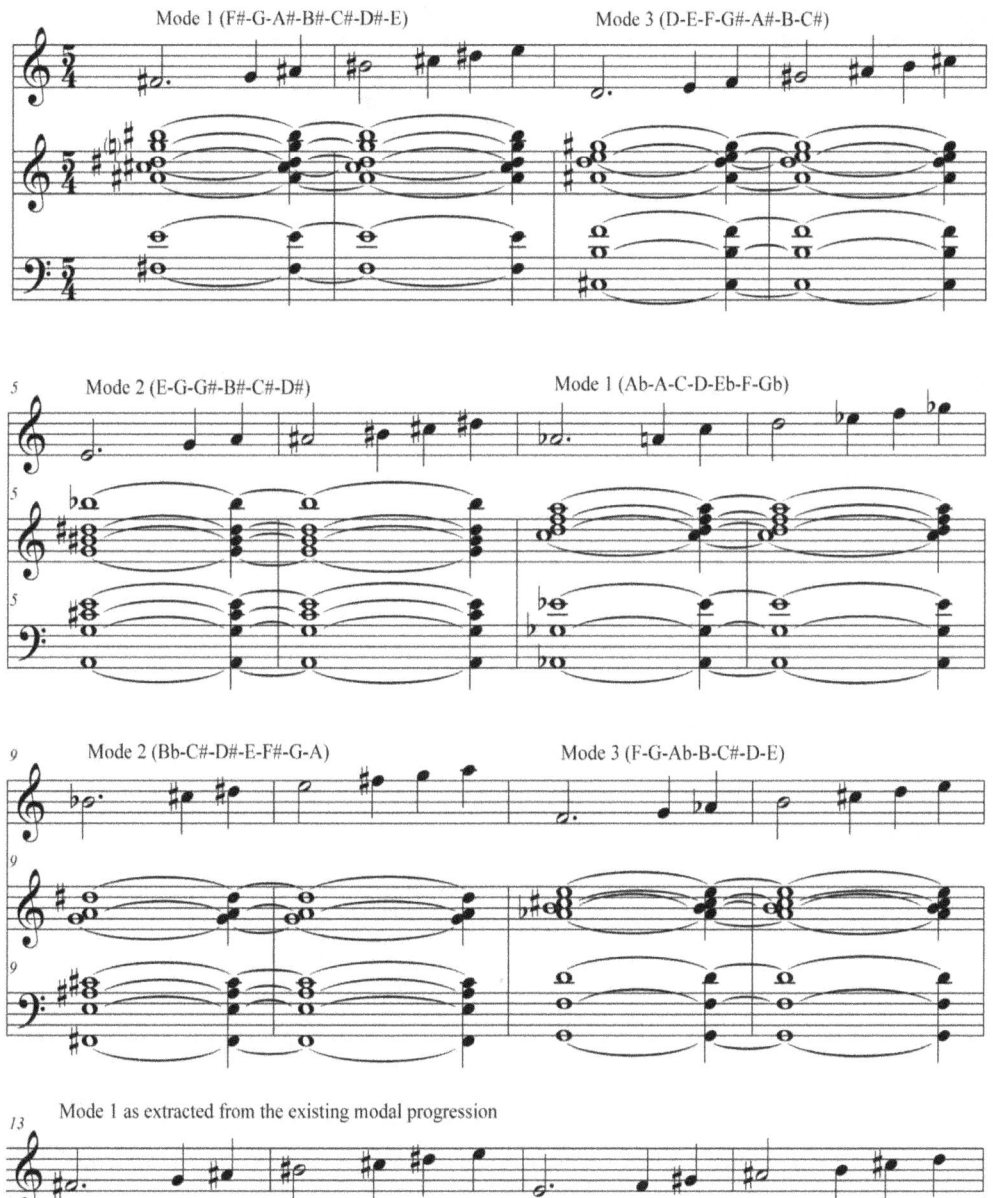

This demonstrates the validity of the entire thesaurus' generation of modes, as each modal construct can be individually used in schematic planning.

Damit erweist sich, dass die Generierung der Modisammlung schlüssig ist, denn jedes modale Konstrukt kann individuell in einer schematischen Planung benutzt werden.

5) FOUR METHODS OF MODAL EXTENSION

5a) SUPERIMPOSITION OF A SYMMETRICAL FIGURE

I will now illustrate how one can utilize symmetrical figures superimposed over an existing symmetrical axis. Say for example that we have a pentatonic mode built around the tritone *D-G#*. The mode has the formula *I-II-#IV-#V-VI*.

By superimposing a symmetrical figure over *D* and then *G#* we have the possibility to extend the mode with related notes. These notes can be freely chosen however must utilize the established symmetrical axis and must be symmetrically constructed. An example can be as little as two notes over each symmetrical axis or as much as one wishes, even up to an endless string of notes. Nicolas Slonimsky has written the "Thesaurus of Scales and Melodic Figures" with many examples of such figures.

The above mode would read as such: *D-E-G#-A#-B*. A superimposed symmetrical figure could be as simple as *D-Eb-G#-A*.

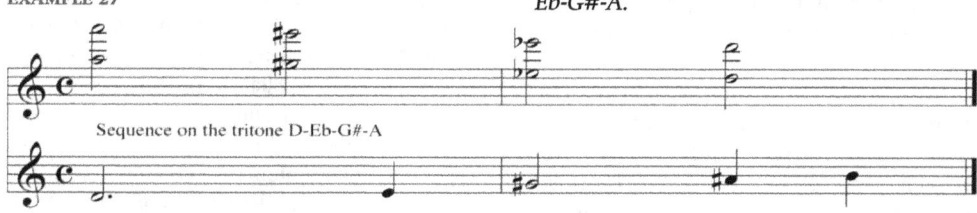

EXAMPLE 27
Sequence on the tritone D-Eb-G#-A
Mode I-II-#IV-#V-VI

This is a simple and direct superimposition. One can as well take the figure and invert the intervallic relationship from *G#* giving us a variant for example. *D-Eb-G#-G*

EXAMPLE 28
Inverted sequence on D-G# (D-Eb-G#-G)
Mode I-II-#IV-#V-VI

Both of these figures are for me superimposed symmetrical extensions.

5) VIER METHODEN MODALER ERWEITERUNG

5a) DIE ÜBERLAGERUNG SYMMETRISCHER FIRGUREN

Es besteht die Möglichkeit, symmetrische Figuren über eine Symmetrieachse zu schichten. Nehmen wir an, wir haben einen pentatonischen Modus um den Tritonus *D-G#* konstruiert, dem die folgende Formel zugrunde liegt: *I-II-#IV-#V-VI*.

Durch die Überlagerung einer symmetrischen Figur über D und dann über G# wird es möglich, den Modus mit verwandten Tönen zu erweitern. Diese Töne können frei gewählt werden, müssen aber zwei Bedingungen erfüllen: Sie müssen auf der bereits zugrunde gelegten Symmetrieachse aufbauen und selbst symmetrisch konstruiert sein. Es können zwei Töne pro Achsialton gewählt werden oder aber soviele wie gewünscht, bis zu einer nicht enden wollenden Reihe von Tönen. Nicolas Slonimsky hat in seinem Buch Thesaurus of Scales and Melodic Patterns eine große Sammlung solcher Figuren aufgeschrieben.

Zurück zu unserem Beispiel. Unser pentatonischer Modus wäre also *D-E-G#-A#-H*. Eine überlagerte symmetrische Figur kann ganz einfach sein wie *D-Eb-G#-A*.

Genauso ist es möglich, die Intervallbeziehungen auf G# umzukehren, was uns eine Variante beschert, die überlagert werden kann: *D-Eb-G#-G*

Hier zwei Beispiele für überlagerte symmetrische Erweiterungen.

One other variant would be to substitute an augmented triad because of its symmetrical relationship to the tritone and build an elaborate figure based on graduated major thirds. An example in letters would be *D-F-E-Ab-Db-C* and now I will transpose and invert the figure on the major third *F#-D#-E-C-G-G#* and then I chose to transpose the figure in its original form once again a major third higher *A#-C#-B#-E-A-G#*.

EXAMPLE 29

Now the cycle is complete. We can use this method vertically or horizontally.

5b) MOTIVIC EXPANSION OF SYMMETRICAL SCALES

With symmetrical scales we can extend a given scale with a motive built upon each pitch. Each separate step receives the same motive or an inversion of the motive upon its various tones. The symmetrical scale could be a sequence upon the tritone. (see the Thesaurus "Partially Transposable Symmetrical Scales") The scale reads in Roman Numerals as such, I-bII-II-III-#IV-V-#V-bVII. Then we can interpolate a figure upon each pitch generating a row of related pitches. With "C" as the starting pitch I will demonstrate an example. *C-(D#-E-G-Ab) Db-(Bb-A-Gb-F) D-(E#-F#-A-Bb) E-(G-G#-B-C) F#-(D#-D-B-A#) G-(A#-B-D-Eb) Ab-(F-E-Db-C) Bb-(C#-D-F-Gb).*

EXAMPLE 30

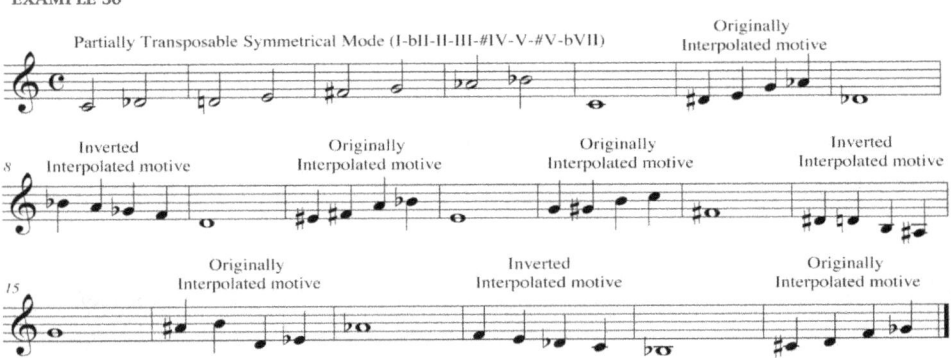

Within each five note combination it is not necessary to play the notes in succession. This method can, as well, utilize scales with the property of a musical unity. The Dorian scale is an example of this (See chapter 8) and a variation could read as such.

Dabei ist es nicht zwingend notwendig, innerhalb jeder Kombinationsgruppe die fünf Töne streng nach Reihenfolge zu spielen. Man kann auch Skalen nutzen, die „musikalische Einheiten" beinhalten. Die dorische Skala ist ein Beispiel hierfür (siehe Kapitel 8) und eine Variation sieht so aus:

EXAMPLE 31

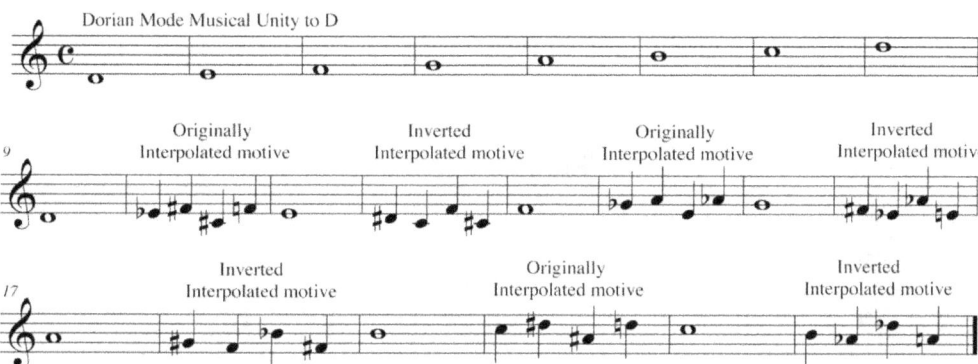

Also the variant of scales creating an inversion on the tritone or augmented triad can be brought into this technique, (See chapter 11) and here is also an example.

Auch Skalen, die durch Umkehrung auf dem Tritonus oder dem übermäßigen Dreiklang entstehen, können in dieser Technik verwendet werden (siehe Kapitel 11):

EXAMPLE 32

5c) CANTUS SYMMETRICUS AND THE TWELVE TONE ROW

Here I have a chain of modes lineally connected through their logical transpositional relationships.

5c) CANTUS SYMMETRICUS UND DIE ZWÖLFTONREIHE

Hier folgt eine Zusammenstellung von Modi, die linear durch ihre logische Transposition miteinander verbunden sind.

EXAMPLE 33

These modes form a structured matrix upon one can write, as well, a superimposed twelve-tone technique. A twelve note row is because of its symmetric structure to an octave, without an audibly dominant pitch.

Interesting enough one has the perfect equality of notes as practiced in the twelve-tone technique and for example, a bass voice utilizing the chaining together of modes connected with the basic principle of controlled transposition as stated in the beginning of the theory.

Diese Modi bilden eine geordnete Matrix, auf der man Musik in einer Zwölftontechnik überlagern kann. Eine Zwölftonreihe hat in sich aufgrund ihrer symmetrischen Struktur keinen hörbaren dominanten Ton.

Äußerst interessant ist die Kombination einerseits aus perfekter Gleichwertigkeit der Töne, wie sie in der Zwölftontechnik praktiziert wird, und andererseits zum Beispiel einem Bass, der verkettete Modi benutzt, wie sie zu Beginn meiner Theorie dargelegt wurde.

CANTUS SYMMETRICUS

EXAMPLE 34

The twelve-tone technique can of course be transposed as wished and built out of the notes from the given motives of a given piece. Therewith one can be assured of a motivic and harmonic unity. We can as well take the modal structures and build harmonies and superimpose the existing twelve tone rows.

Die Zwölftonreihe kann natürlich nach Wunsch transponiert werden, genauso kann ein Motiv aus einem Musikstück für die Auswahl der zu verwendenden Töne oder Phrasen Pate stehen. So erlangt man motivische und harmonische Einheitlichkeit. Natürlich können Harmonien auch der modalen Struktur entstammen und von Zwölftonreihen überlagert werden.

CANTUS SYMMETRICUS PART 2

EXAMPLE 35

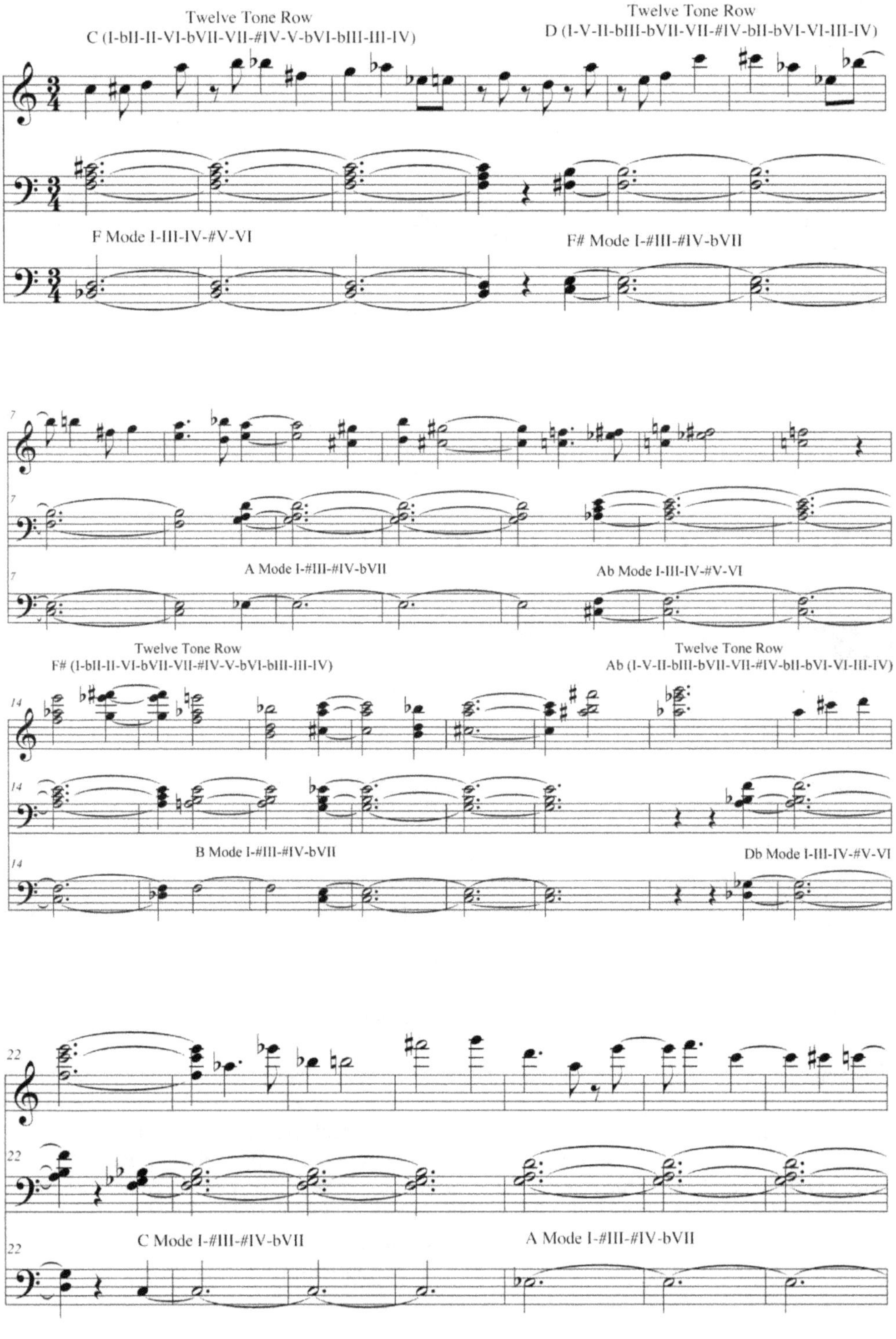

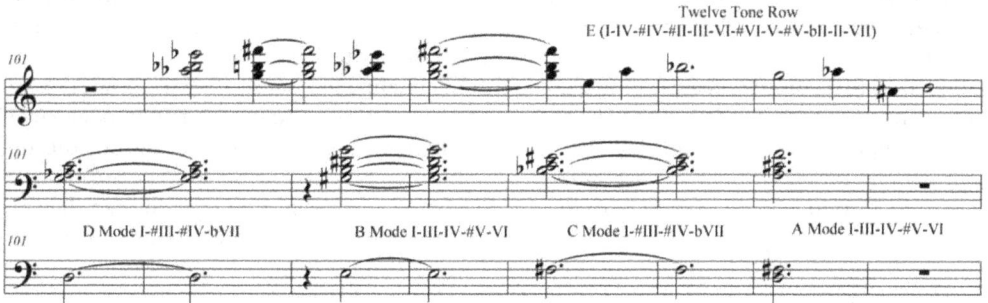

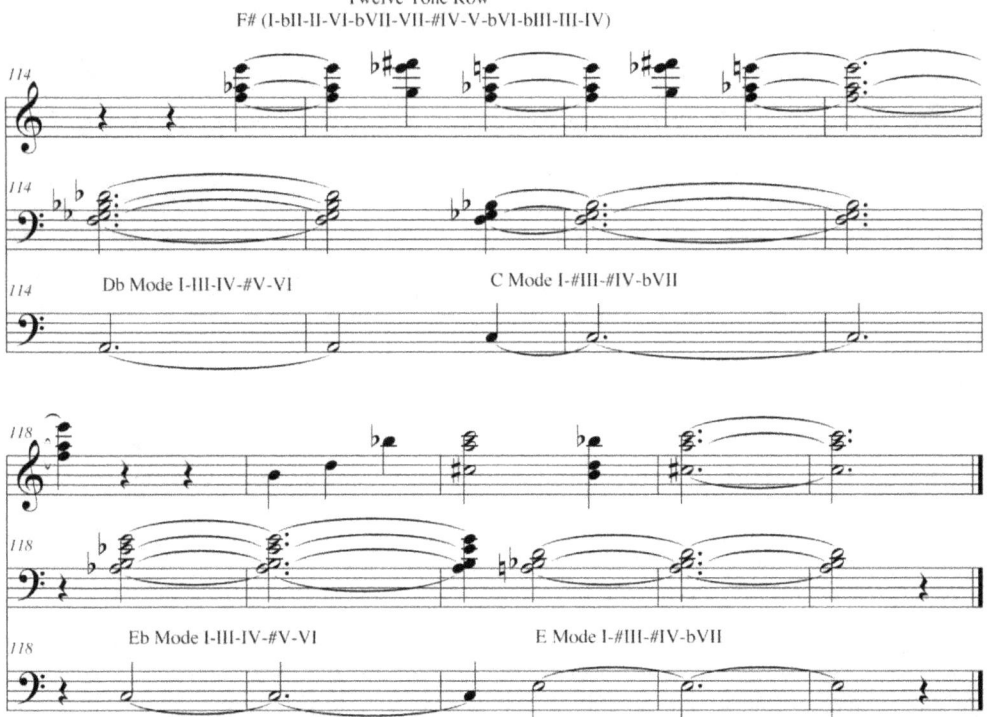

At this point it is important to mention that all forms of superimposition with an unequal symmetrical mode bring about a coexistence of two or more elements. Musical unities, symmetrical generations or twelve-tone rows needn't simply be reserved for the upper voices. We can bring them into play in any register we wish. I will now for example show how Example 35 can look otherwise.

Ein wichtiger Hinweis an dieser Stelle: Alle Formen der Überlagerung mit einem ungleich verteilten Modus bringen eine Koexistenz von zwei oder mehr Elementen hervor. Musikalische Einheiten, symmetrische Konstrukte oder Zwölftonreihen sind nicht zwangsläufig auf die oberen Stimmen beschränkt. Sie können ausnahmslos in jeder Tonlage zum Einsatz kommen. Beispiel 35 klingt unter diesem Aspekt etwas anders:

CANTUS SYMMETRICUS PART 3

EXAMPLE 35 a

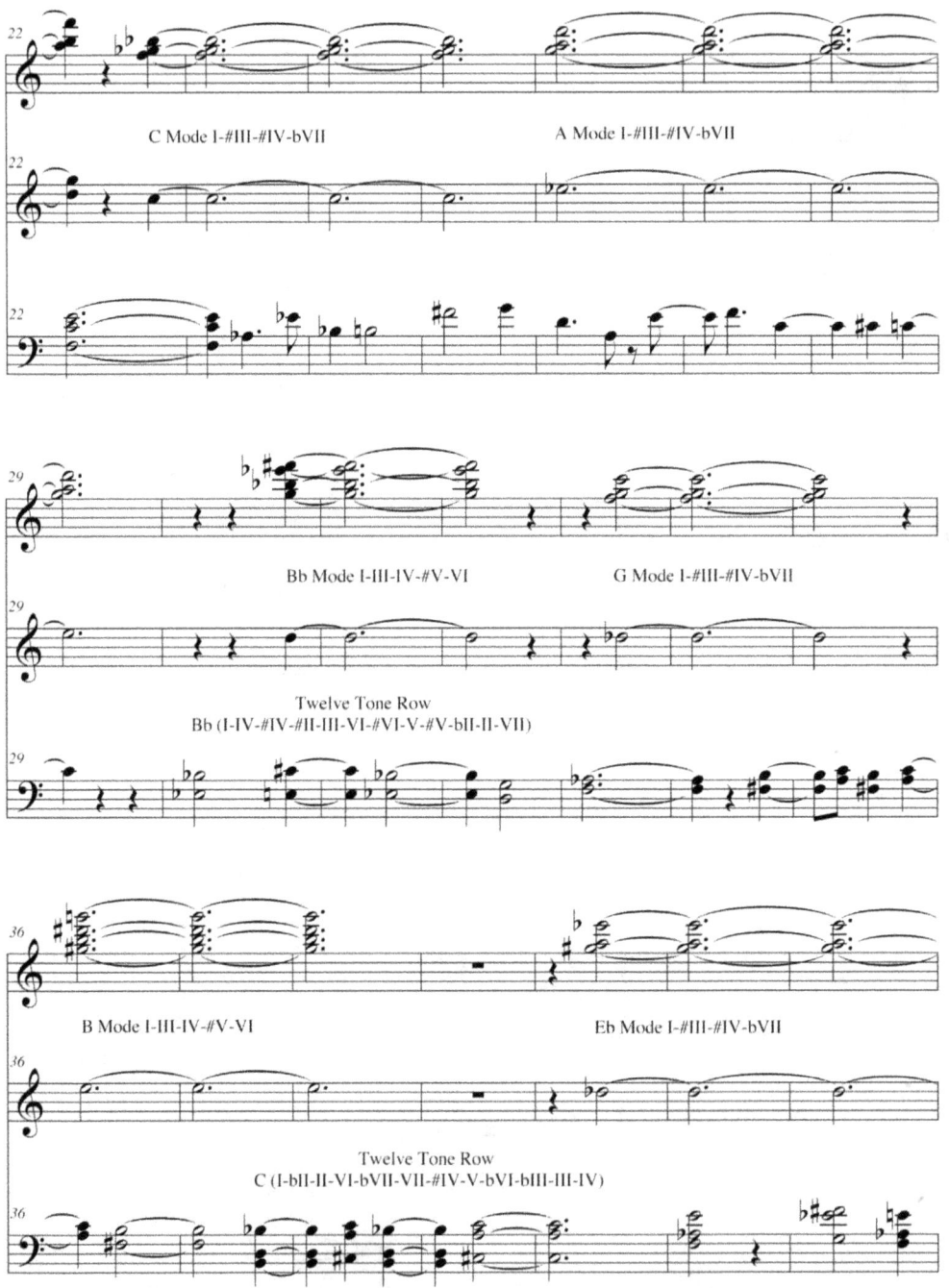

5d) POLYMODAL EXTENSION AS PRACTICED IN MODERN JAZZ

Many times I truly wondered where McCoy Tyner's 70ties music derived its notes from. A very clear example would be looking at the undertoning of fourths where the usual blues scale would be for example in Cminor.

An example looks as such. C with a fourth underneath it, G and once again then D. If we have a blues melody *C-Eb-F-Gb-F* then the combination will be triads built in fourths playing three modes at once. *D-G-C; F-Bb-Eb; G-C-F; Ab-Db-Gb; G-C-F.*

EXAMPLE 36

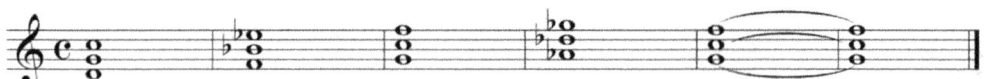

One can as well make quadrads with this technique. *Db-E-A-C; E-G-C-Eb; Gb-A-D-F; G-Bb-Eb-Gb; Gb-A-D-F;*

EXAMPLE 37

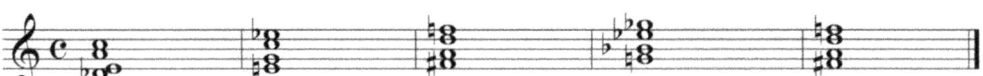

This polymodal technique can as well base itself on given triads that may appear even in complex structures. An example could be a *C7b9-#11-6* chord. The three notes at the top of the chord form an *F#minor* chord. One can use exactly the same technique with polymodal extension over F#minor and therefore over the *C7b9-#11-6* chord.

EXAMPLE 38

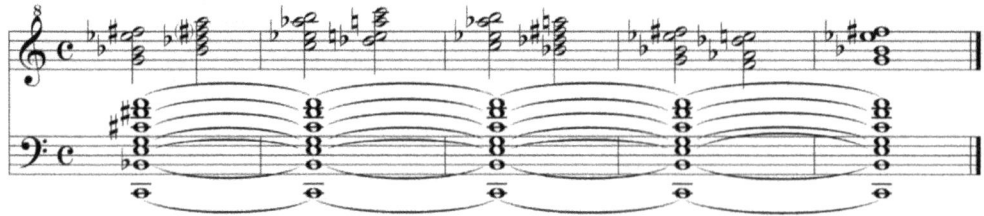

| A very simple example is the *CMAJ7* chord. It has as well inclusive with the third, fifth and seventh, the triad Eminor in its basic structure. It is practiced often that a jazz musician improvises Eminor blues over the *CMAJ7* chord. | Ein sehr einfaches Beispiel aus der Praxis ist der CMAJ7 Akkord. In seinem Grundaufbau befindet sich mit der Terz, der Quinte und der Septime der volle E-Moll-Dreiklang. Oft hört man einen Jazzmusiker E-Moll-Blues über CMAJ7 improvisieren. |

EXAMPLE 38a

The expression "free blowing" came to be as a technique using a collection of various resources that all circulated to a central pitch. One method could be a bassist playing a riff based on a blues scale or perhaps on a mixolydian mode. Each of these riffs would define a scale starting from "C". Then a pianist or saxophonist could play another mode against the blues or mixolydian mode however this mode would also have a "C" within it.

One of the more common resources is the usage of the traditional Church Modes. Each Church Mode must start on "C". All of the resulting Church Modes are in this sense related. One can as well then start to alter triads out of each Church Mode and derive a polymodal blues as was formerly discussed, over the entire structure.

Der Ausdruck „free blowing" beschreibt eine Technik, die immer einen Zentralton im Blick behält. Ein Beispiel ist ein Basssatz, der einen Blues-Riff darstellt oder eine mixolydische Figur. Jeder Riff wird als C-Skala gespielt. Dann kann ein Pianist oder Saxophonist einen anderen Modus spielen, er muss aber ein C enthalten. Jazzmusiker nutzen hierfür gerne Kirchenmodi. Wenn diese mit C beginnen, in diesem Sinne also eine Verwandtschaft aufweisen, können sie problemlos in den polymodalen Blues integriert werden.

68

This technique must not come out of the blues and can be used with non-diatonic scales as well.

Diese Art polymodalischer Erweiterung ist nicht auf den Blues beschränkt, auch nicht-diatonische Modi können verwendet werden.

EXAMPLE 39a

The Generation of a Non-Diatonic Scale using the same Procedure

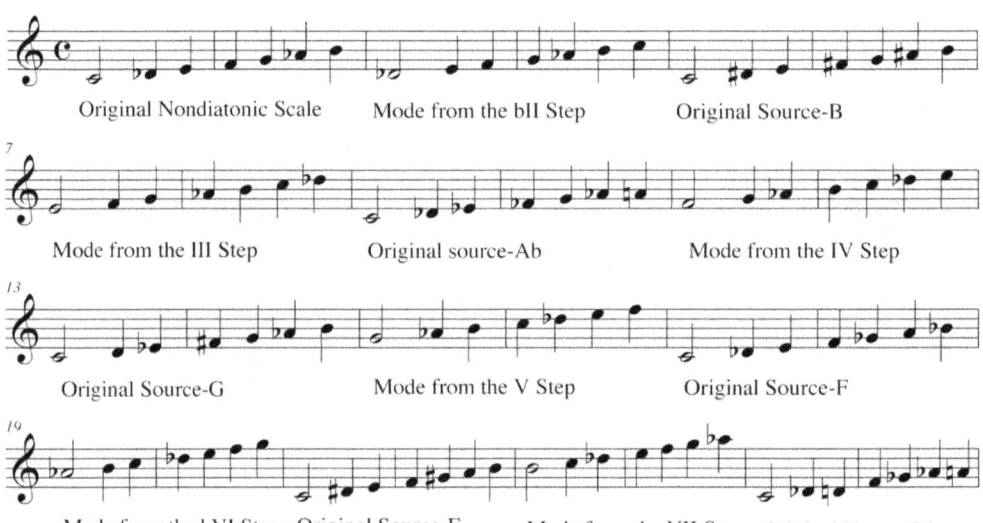

IMPROVISACIÓN de los GITANOS

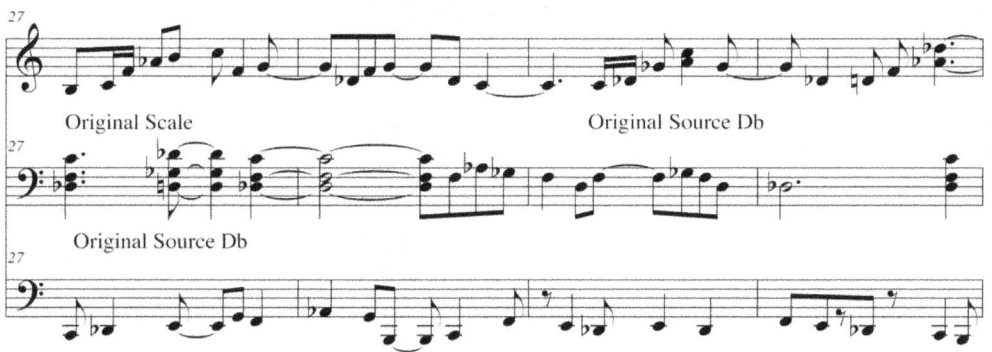

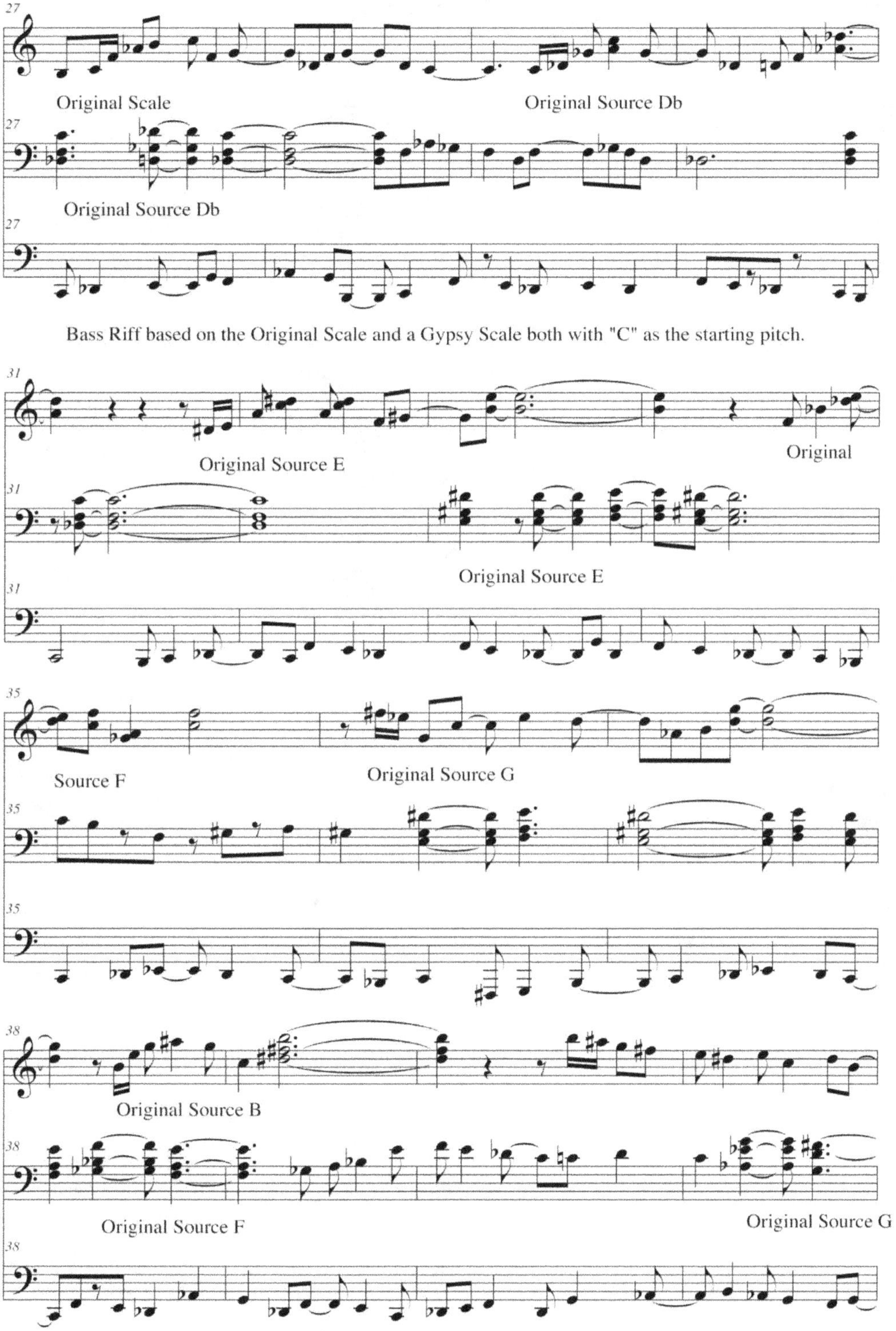
27
Original Scale
Original Source Db
27
Original Source Db
27
Bass Riff based on the Original Scale and a Gypsy Scale both with "C" as the starting pitch.
31
Original Source E
Original
31
Original Source E
31
35
Source F
Original Source G
35
35
38
Original Source B
38
Original Source F
Original Source G
38

6) A NEW DODECAPHONY THROUGH THE USAGE OF POLYMODALITY AND ADJACENT MODES

One of the basic principles of the twelve-tone technique is the utilization of all twelve chromatic pitches before the repetition of the first. Therefore one constructs twelve-tone rows for the execution of this concept. Therewith we receive the perfect equality of pitches resulting in an atonal environment.

At one point I decided to build a series of polymodal structures resulting in the usage of all twelve half-steps. Because of my symmetrical thinking, as presented in the theory, we can rethink the building of a twelve-tone environment.

One clear example is to choose a heptatonic mode, and superimpose a "sister mode" upon the other symmetrical axis. This mode would be as well a heptatonic mode and in the case of the tritone, is built upon the augmented fourth of the original mode. Also the "sister mode" should consist of the five pitches which are not found in the original mode. An example in letters would be as such. *C-Db-E-F#-G-A-Bb* is the original mode. The polymodal "sister mode" is built as such, *F#-G#-B-B#-D-D#-E#*.

6) EINE NEUE DODEKAPHONIE DURCH POLYMODALITÄT UND SICH ERGÄNZENDE MODI

Eines der Grundprinzipien der Zwölftontechnik ist, dass erst alle zwölf chromatischen Töne erklungen sein müssen, bevor sich der erste Ton wiederholt. Für die Ausführbarkeit dieses Konzeptes werden Zwölftonreihen erstellt. Man erhält Gebilde mit gleichberechtigten Tönen, was zu einer atonalen Umgebung führt.

Eines Tages entschied ich mich, eine Reihe polymodaler Strukturen zu schaffen, die den Gebrauch aller zwölf Halbtöne vorsieht. Da ich in Symmetrien denke, habe ich den Aufbau einer Zwölftonumgebung neu konzipiert.

Für ein anschauliches Beispiel wird ein heptatonischer Modus ausgewählt und ein "Geschwister-Modus" über den zweiten Achsialton gelegt. Dieser zweite Modus soll ebenfalls ein heptatonischer sein – ist der zweite Achsialton ein Tritonus, so ist der zweite Modus auf der übermäßigen Quarte des Original-Modus aufgebaut. Der „Geschwister-Modus" sollte außerdem jene fünf Töne enthalten, die im Original-Modus nicht zu finden sind. Ausgeschrieben lautet dies so: *C-Db-E-F#-G-A-B* ist die Original-Modalität. Dazu die polymodale „Geschwister-Modalität": *F#-G#-H-H#-D-D#-E*

EXAMPLE 40

When I apply this technique I purposely leave the F# and B# out of the sister mode because this tritone is already in the original mode. The result is a twelve-tone structure.

I personally reserve registers for each mode which brings the dichotomy into this technique. We can with a transpositional scheme order each modal transposition through the ordering of a given symmetrical axis as proposed in the opening of my theory and at the same time we can exercise the principles of dodecaphony. When the original mode is used as a sound chamber and the sister mode as a melody one can clearly hear a logical harmonic movement through the structured symmetrical axes.

Wenn ich diese Technik anwende, klammere ich absichtlich F# und H# aus dem „Geschwister-Modus" aus, denn dieser Tritonus ist schon im Original-Modus enthalten. Das Ergebnis ist eine Zwölftonstruktur. Verteile ich die Modi nun in verschiedene Register, passiert etwas Zweideutiges mit der Musik.

Diese neue Dodekaphonie ermöglicht gleichzeitig die Einhaltung der Prinzipien der Zwölftontechnik und die durch die symmetrische Achse gesicherten geordneten Transpositionen nach einem dafür erstellten Schema. Wenn der Ausgangsmodus als Klangraum und der „Geschwister-Modus" als Melodiequelle genutzt wird, kann man klar und deutlich eine logische harmonische Bewegung durch die strukturierten symmetrischen Achsen hören.

DODECAPHONIC EUPHONICS

EXAMPLE 41

In a contrapunctal approach the same result is possible when the two modal structures maintain their identity.

In einer kontrapunktischen Annäherung ist das gleiche Ergebnis möglich, solange die beiden modalen Konstrukte ihre Identität bewahren.

DODECAPHONIC EUPHONICS PART 2

EXAMPLE 42

Also in a non-polymodal environment we can have adjacent hexatonic modes which in total form a twelve-tone row. An example of this in the literature is the String Trio Opus 45 from Arnold Schönberg.

In einer nicht-polymodalen Umgebung haben wir es mit sich ergänzenden hexatonischen Modi zu tun, die zusammen eine Zwölftonreihe ergeben. Ein Beispiel dafür aus der Literatur ist das Streichertrio op. 45 von Arnold Schönberg.

EXAMPLE 43

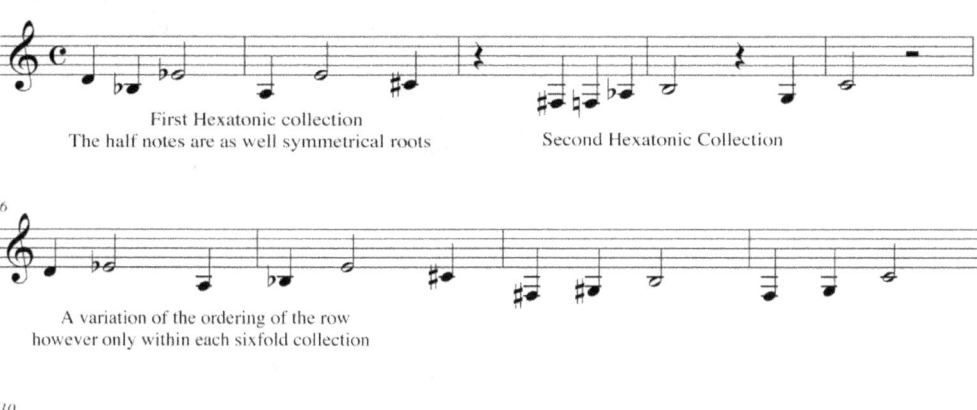

Also within the realm of adjacent modes we can place any combination of modes together resulting in no repetition of a given pitch. For example a hexatonic next to another hexatonic, a heptatonic next to a pentatonic or an octatonic next to a quadratonic etc. When we have modes based on unequal distribution to a symmetrical axis, then each movement of a mode will be heard as a nonstatic event.

Im Reich der sich ergänzenden Modi können wir jede nur denkbare modale Kombination zusammenstellen, solange sich kein Ton wiederholt. Eine hexatonische neben einer anderen hexatonischen Modalität, eine heptatonische neben einer pentatonischen oder wenn möglich eine oktatonische neben einer quadratonischen. Wenn wir Modi haben, die eine ungleiche Verteilung um eine gewisse symmetrische Achse aufzeigen, ist jede modale Bewegung als ein nicht statisches Ergebnis zu hören.

EXAMPLE 44

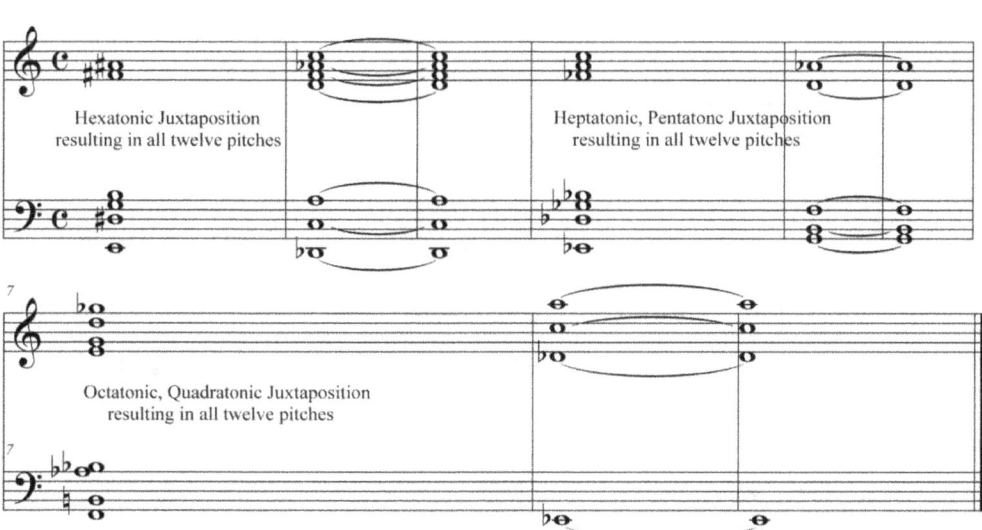

7) THESAURUS OF SYMMETRICAL TWELVE-TONE ROWS

In addition to this new dodecaphony, with the application of polymodal constructions of two modes built upon the tritone, we can also construct symmetrical twelve-tone rows which can be as well superimposed upon the original mode.

7) SAMMLUNG SYMMETRISCHER ZWÖLFTONREIHEN

Bei der neuen Dodekaphonie kommen die polymodalen Konstrukte zweier auf dem Tritonus aufbauender Modi zur Anwendung. Alternativ dazu kann man auch symmetrische Zwölftonskalen bilden, die auf die gleiche Weise über den Ausgangsmodus gelagert werden können.

EXAMPLE 45 — Symmetrical twelve tone rows beginning on "C"

We needn't utilize symmetrical twelve-tone rows but these rows give as well the effect of a pure symmetrical generation and have therefore a separate ordering beyond simply a freely constructed twelve-tone row. As already explained we have also the possibility to juxtapose two hexatonic modes or other combinations which theoretically also create a twelve-tone row and superimpose these special structures.

Es besteht keine Pflicht, solche Zwölftonskalen anzuwenden, doch auch diese Reihen erzeugen den Effekt einer symmetrischen Generierung und haben demnach eine eigene Ordnung im Gegensatz zu einer frei zusammengestellten Zwölftonreihe. Wie schon beschrieben ist es auch möglich, zwei hexatonische Modi oder andere sich ergänzende Kombinationen nebeneinander zu stellen, die dadurch eine Zwölftonskala bilden und als solche überlagert werden können.

Firstly I will demonstrate various hexatonic juxtapositions creating various twelve-tone rows and then I will develop harmonies from the resulting unequally distributed modes and superimpose a collection of three various symmetrical twelve-tone rows.

Als Erstes werden hier verschiedene, sich ergänzende hexatonische Modalitäten gezeigt, die unterschiedliche Zwölftonskalen bilden. Aus den sich so ergebenden ungleich verteilten Modi entwickeln wir Harmonien. Danach können wir eine Auswahl von drei symmetrischen Zwölf-Ton-Skalen überlagern.

EXAMPLE 45 a

SYMMETRICAL DODECAPHONY

EXAMPLE 46

Now I will list these special symmetrical twelve-tone structures with Roman numerals for the facility of transposition in a thesaurus.

One can substitute members matching as tritones or major thirds in regards to the augmented triad and create variants of these intervallic sequences.

An dieser Stelle folgt eine Sammlung dieser speziellen symmetrischen Zwölftonstrukturen, notiert in römischen Ziffern, um die Transposition zu erleichtern. Man kann einzelne Stufen, die als Tritonus oder Durterzen des übermäßigen Dreiklangs zusammenpassen, gegeneinander austauschen und so Variationen der hier vorgestellten Intervallsequenzen herstellen.

Mit gekennzeichneten Tritoni:

I-**bII**-bVI-bIII-III-IV-#IV-**V**-II-VI-bVII-VII
I-**V**-bVI-bIII-III-IV-#IV-**bII**-II-VI-bVII-VII

For example
I-**bII**-bVI-bIII-III-IV-#IV-**V**-II-VI-bVII-VII
I-**V**-bVI-bIII-III-IV-#IV-**bII**-II-VI-bVII-VII

and an example with major thirds in substitution.
I-**IV**-II-bIII-III-**VI**-#IV-V-#V-**bII**-bVII-VII
I-**VI**-II-bIII-III-**bII**-#IV-V-#V-**IV**-bVII-VII.

Once again we can choose unequally distributed modes which as well possess these pitch arrangements. Therewith we can work with motives from both the modes and the symmetrical twelve-tone rows and create a homogenous environment.

Mit gekennzeichneten Durterzen als übermäßigen Dreiklängen:

I-**IV**-II-bIII-III-**VI**-#IV-V-#V-**bII**-bVII-VII
I-**VI**-II-bIII-III-**bII**-#IV-V-#V-**IV**-bVII-VII.

Wiederum haben wir die Wahl, uns für ungleich verteilte Modi, die dieselben Tonarrangements besitzen, zu entscheiden. Auf diese Art können wir mit Motiven arbeiten, die sowohl den Modi als auch den symmetrischen Zwölftonskalen entspringen. Das schafft eine homogene Klangumgebung.

7b) SYMMETRICAL TWELVE-TONE ROWS – BASED ON THE TRITONE

I-bII-bVI-bIII-III-IV-#IV-V-II-VI-bVII-VII
I-bII-II-VI-III-IV-#IV-V-bVI-bIII-bVII-VII
I-bII-II-bIII-bVII-IV-#IV-V-bVI-VI-III-VII
I-bII-II-bIII-III-VII-#IV-V-bVI-VI-bVII-IV
I-V-II-bIII-III-IV-#IV-bII-bVI-VI-bVII-VII
I-V-bVI-bIII-III-IV-#IV-bII-II-VI-bVII-VII
I-bII-bVI-VI-III-IV-#IV-V-II-bIII-bVII-VII
I-bII-II-VI-bVII-IV-#IV-V-bVI-bIII-III-VII
I-V-II-VI-III-IV-#IV-bII-bVI-bIII-bVII-VII
I-V-II-bIII-bVII-IV-#IV-bII-bVI-VI-III-VII
I-V-II-bIII-III-VII-#IV-bII-bVI-VI-bVII-IV
I-bII-bVI-bIII-bVII-IV-#IV-V-II-VI-III-VII
I-bII-bVI-bIII-III-IV-#IV-V-II-VI-bVII-VII
I-bII-II-VI-bVII-IV-#IV-V-bVI-bIII-III-VII

I-bII-II-bIII-bVII-VII-#IV-V-bVI-VI-III-IV
I-V-bVI-VI-III-IV-#IV-bII-II-bIII-bVII-VII
I-V-II-VI-bVII-IV-#IV-bII-bVI-bIII-III-VII
I-V-II-bIII-bVII-VII-#IV-bII-bVI-VI-III-IV
I-V-bVI-bIII-bVII-IV-#IV-bII-II-VI-III-VII
I-V-bVI-bIII-bVII-VII-#IV-bII-II-VI-bVII-IV
I-V-II-VI-III-VII-#IV-bII-bVI-bIII-bVII-IV
I-bII-bVI-VI-bVII-IV-#IV-V-II-bIII-III-VII
I-bII-bVI-VI-III-IV-#IV-V-II-bIII-bVII-IV
I-bII-bVI-bIII-bVII-VII-#IV-V-II-VI-III-IV
I-bII-II-VI-bVII-VII-#IV-V-bVI-bIII-III-IV
I-V-bVI-VI-bVII-IV-#IV-bII-II-bIII-III-VII
I-V-II-VI-bVII-VII-#IV-bII-bVI-bIII-III-IV
I-bII-bVI-VI-bVII-VII-#IV-V-II-bIII-III-IV

BASED ON THE AUGMENTED TRIAD

I-IV-II-bIII-III-VI-#IV-V-#V-bII-bVII-VII
I-bII-#IV-bIII-III-IV-bVII-V-#V-VI-II-VII
I-bII-II-V-III-IV-#IV-VII-#V-VI-bVII-bIII
I-VI-II-bIII-III-bII-#IV-V-#V-IV-bVII-VII
I-bII-bVII-bIII-III-IV-II-V-#V-VI-#IV-VII
I-bII-II-VII-III-IV-#IV-bIII-#V-VI-bVII-V
I-IV-#IV-bIII-III-VI-bVII-V-#V-bII-II-VII
I-IV-II-V-III-VI-#IV-VII-#V-bII-bVII-bIII
I-IV-bVII-bIII-III-VI-II-V-#V-bII-#IV-VII
I-IV-II-VII-III-VI-#IV-bIII-#V-bII-bVII-V
I-VI-#IV-bIII-III-bII-bVII-V-#V-IV-II-VII
I-VI-II-V-III-bII-#IV-VII-#V-IV-bVII-bIII
I-VI-bVII-bIII-III-bII-II-V-#V-IV-#IV-VII

I-VI-II-VII-III-bII-#IV-bIII-#V-IV-bVII-V
I-bII-#IV-V-III-IV-bVII-VII-#V-VI-II-bIII
I-bII-bVII-VII-III-IV-II-bIII-#V-VI-#IV-V
I-bII-#IV-VII-III-IV-bVII-bIII-#V-VI-II-V
I-bII-bVII-V-III-IV-II-VII-#V-VI-#IV-bIII
I-IV-#IV-V-III-VI-bVII-VII-#V-bII-II-bIII
I-VI-#IV-V-III-bII-bVII-VII-#V-IV-II-bIII
I-IV-bVII-VII-III-VI-II-bIII-#V-bII-#IV-V
I-VI-bVII-VII-III-bII-II-bIII-#V-IV-#IV-V
I-IV-#IV-VII-III-VI-bVII-bIII-#V-bII-II-V
I-IV-bVII-V-III-VI-II-VII-#V-bII-#IV-bIII
I-VI-#IV-VII-III-bII-bVII-bIII-#V-IV-II-V
I-VI-bVII-V-III-bII-II-VII-#V-IV-#IV-bIII

An interesting resource for juxtaposed hexatonic modes are the highly intriguing collection of Josef Matthias Hauer's 44 Tropen.

One can discover within Hauer's tropes thirteen juxtaposed hexatonic modes which are symmetrical to each other. This technique fascinated me. Hence I industriously discovered many more twelve-tone rows of this sort. Each trope begins with six pitches. The following six are interestingly a retrograde inversion beginning from the final tone. As earlier stated, like in Schoenberg's Opus 45 if these hexatonic combinations remain together one will hear a logical harmonic movement. Additionally because of the symmetrical unity within each of these particular tropes it is possible to superimpose them.

Eine interessante Ressource für sich ergänzende hexatonische Modi ist die eindrucksvolle Sammlung von Josef Matthias Hauers 44 Tropen.

Innerhalb von Hauers Tropen gibt es dreizehn hexatonische ergänzte Modi, die zueinander symmetrisch sind. Diese Technik hat mich fasziniert. Ich habe mich deswegen damit beschäftigt, entsprechende symmetrische Zwölftonreihen zu finden. Jede Trope fängt mit sechs Tönen an. Die folgenden sechs Töne sind eine Krebsumkehrung, beginnend mit dem letzten Ton. Wie vorher erwähnt – wie in Schönbergs Opus 45 – gibt es zwischen den hexatonischen Modi einen klaren harmonischen Wechsel. Außerdem können wegen der symmetrischen Einheit alle Tropen überlagert werden.

Symmetrical Tropes

8) THE USAGE OF MUSICAL UNITIES

Let's begin by explaining what I mean by a musical unity. A musical unity is my description of a perfect inversion to a given note. It is within itself dependent upon this given note and structures derived from this technique, circulate to it. An example could be as simple as a chosen interval that is inverted to a beginning note. This could look as such; C-D followed by C-Bb or C-F followed by C-G.

8) DIE ANWENDUNG MUSIKALISCHER EINHEITEN

Zuerst möchte ich den Begriff „musikalische Einheit" erklären. Eine musikalische Einheit ist die von mir gewählte Bezeichnung für Umkehrungen (Spiegelungen) von einem beliebigen Ausgangston aus. Sie ist also abhängig vom Ausgangston, und die nach dieser Technik abgeleiteten Töne zirkulieren um ihn. Ein einfaches Beispiel, ein Intervall wird auf einem Ausgangston umgekehrt: C-D und in Folge davon C-B, C-F und dazugehörig C-G.

EXAMPLE 47

"C" as the central tone

One can expand this technique as one wishes. An example of a triad would be *C-Eb-B* followed by *C-A* and *Db*.

Diese Technik ist beliebig lange anwendbar. Ein Beispiel für einen Dreiklang: *C-Eb-H*, als Umkehrung *C-A-Db*.

EXAMPLE 48

"C" as central tone

An example of a quadrad could look like this; *C-F-Ab-B* followed by *C-G-E-Db*.

Ein Beispiel für einen Vierklang: *C-F-Ab-H*, als Umkehrung *C-G-E-Db*.

EXAMPLE 49

"C" as central tone

At this point one can create even more related notes by looking at each note of a chosen structure and inverting the structure from each member of the structure. Therefore we can take the above quadradic structure and invert the structure from F, Ab and B. This would give us three other related quadradic structures. *F-Ab-B-*and C would generate *F-D-B-Bb*. *Ab-B-C-F* would generate *Ab-F-E-B*. *B-C-F-Ab* would generate *B-Bb-F-D*.

Je größer der Umfang der Ausgangsstruktur ist, desto mehr verwandte Töne kann man durch Umkehrung generieren, denn nicht nur der Basiston eines Mehrklangs oder der Anfangston einer Tonfolge kann als Spiegelachse fungieren, sondern jeder an der gewählten Struktur beteiligte Ton. In dem zuvor gewählten Vierklang war zunächst F die Spiegelachse, aber auch As und H können als Spiegelachse fungieren. Das ergibt drei weitere verwandte viertönige Strukturen. Aus *F-Ab-H-C* wird *F-D-H-B*, *Ab-H-C-F* ergibt *Ab-F-E-H* und *H-C-F-Ab* wird zu *H-B-F-D*.

EXAMPLE 50

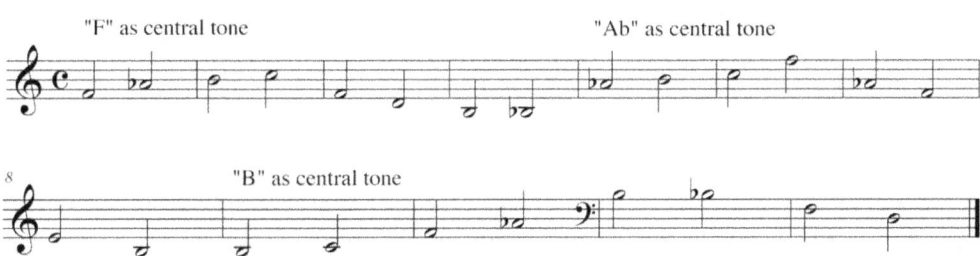

As in my entire technique we can either use these structures lineally or harmonically.

This form of hybrid generation actually is an infinite variational technique that can generate a never-ending row of related notes. I will firstly demonstrate a generation of inversions originating with the major triad.

Auch diese Technik lässt sich horizontal wie vertikal anwenden. Diese Form der Hybrid-Erzeugung bietet unendlich viele Variationen, die eine nicht enden wollende Menge verwandter Klänge hervorbringen können. Hier eine Demonstration mit einem Durdreiklang zu Beginn:

EXAMPLE 51

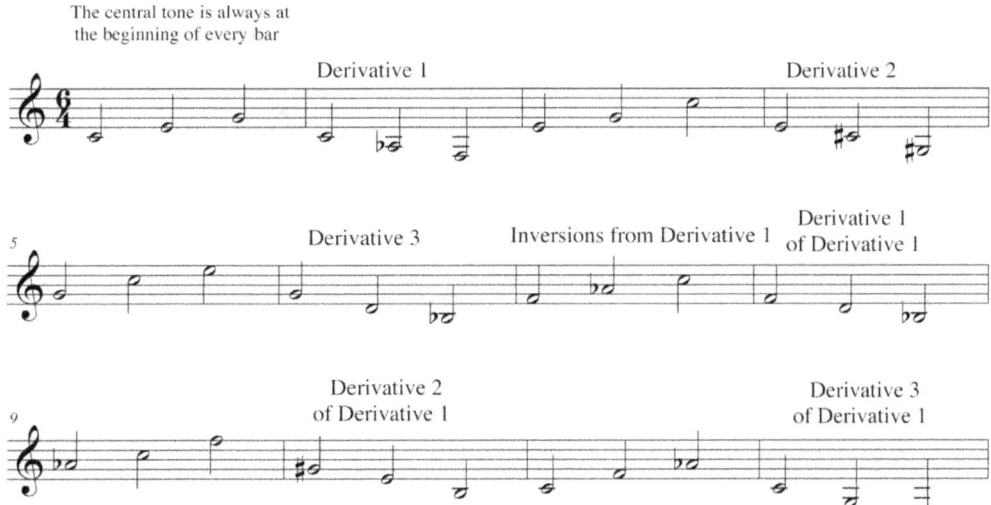

Now I will once again generate further inversions with the quadrad *C-F-Ab-B*.

Und hier erzeugen wir weitere Umkehrungen mit dem Vierklang *C-F-Ab-H*.

EXAMPLE 52

We must simply, with each newly generated structure, continue to derive newer combinations by always inverting upon its different members. This form of inverted note derivation is audible in that our perception automatically recognizes symmetrical forms.

This form of pitch formation can as well be used for superimposition over transpositional schemes utilizing the modes found in my thesaurus. (See chapter 3)

Man muss einfach mit jeder neu erzeugten Stellung fortfahren, weitere Kombinationen zu bilden, indem man die einzelnen Stufen als Spiegelachse nutzt. Die durch Umkehrung hergeleiteten Klänge werden vom Gehör automatisch als symmetrische Formen erkannt.

Diese Klangbildung kann auch mit den Transpositionsschemata der Modi überlagert werden (siehe Kapitel 3).

SYMMETRISCHE GENERIERUNG

EXAMPLE 53

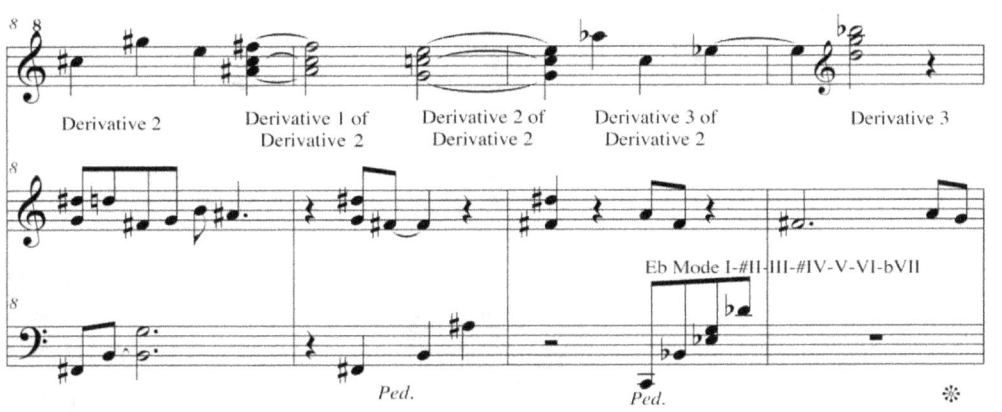

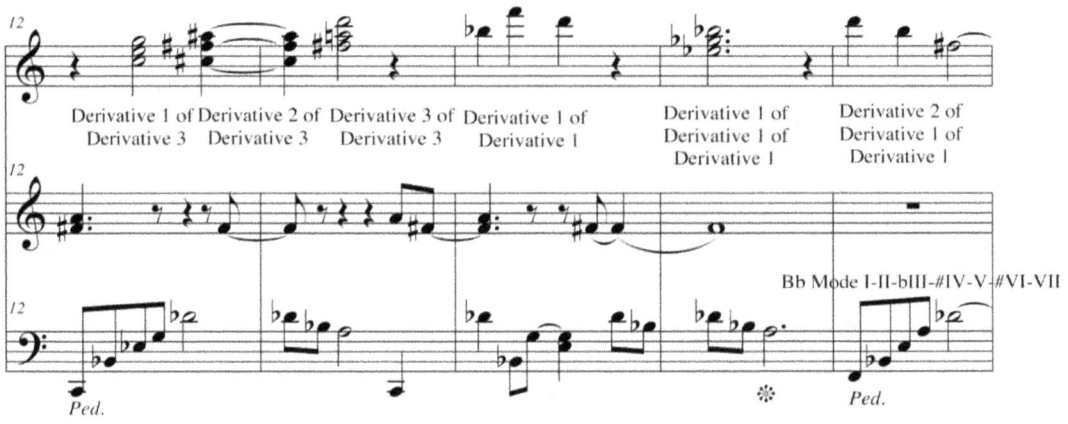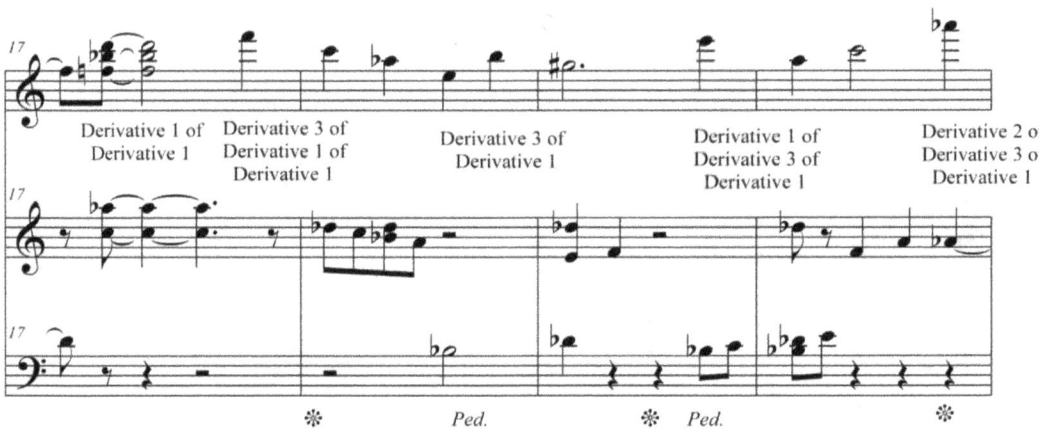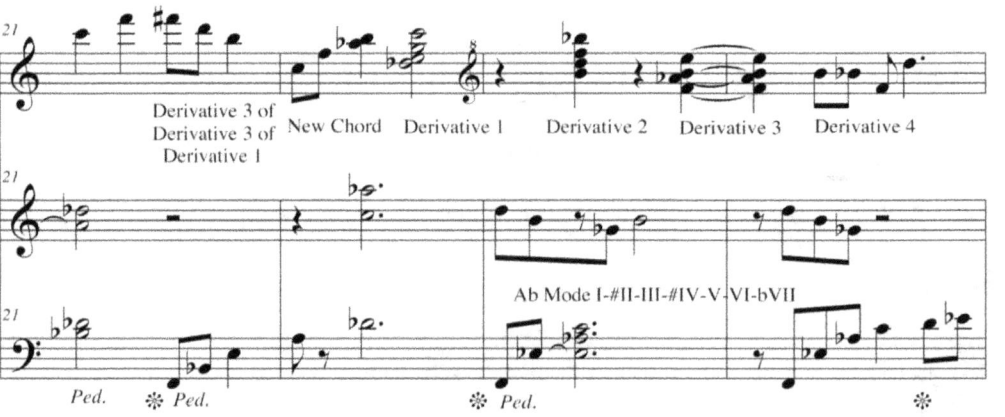

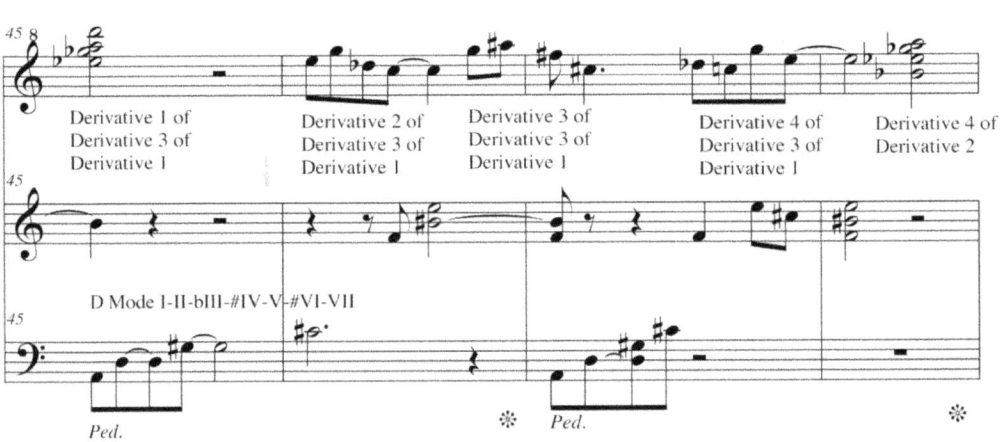

In this thinking method it is also possible to bring the symmetrically constructed structures as sequences on the tritone and augmented triad into this form of usage.

Auf diese Weise können auch symmetrisch konstruierte Strukturen wie Sequenzen auf dem Tritonus oder übermäßigen Dreiklang verwendet werden.

SYMMETRISCHE GENERIERUNG TEIL 2

105

Because of their symmetrical construction they can coexist with musical unities. One can truly develop independently the schematics of these musical unities. We can also conceive transpositional schemes, perhaps related to the scheme of the original modal transposition and as well superimpose these structures.

Aufgrund ihres symmetrischen Aufbaus können diese Strukturen mit musikalischen Einheiten koexistieren. Man kann die Funktionsweise der musikalischen Einheiten unabhängig entwickeln oder Transpositionsschemata ersinnen, auch mit dem Schema der ursprünglichen modalen Transpositionen verwandte, und die sich daraus ergebenden Töne überlagern.

SYMMETRISCHE GENERIERUNG TEIL 3

EXAMPLE 55

The effect is that of what one might expect. Because of the inner unity of such structures they will ring independently from the chosen transposable modes and will not interfere with the independence of the modes themselves. aWWWThis occurs because the unequally distributed modes have a dominant pitch, the symmetrical root and a musical unity circulates to its central tone. We can as well utilize the symmetrical axis of a given mode, as earlier stated in my paper on modal extension, as our home-base for the superimposition. (see Chapter 5)

Der klangliche Effekt entspricht wohl den Erwartungen. Wegen der inneren Einheit solcher Stellungen erklingen sie unabhängig von den gewählten transponierbaren Modi und stören deren Struktur nicht. Dies erklärt sich dadurch, dass die ungleich verteilten Modi einen Grundton besitzen und die musikalischen Einheiten einen zentralen Ton. Ebenso kann man die symmetrische Achse eines vorgegebenen Modus als Ausgangsbasis für die Überlagerung verwenden, wie schon zuvor in Kapitel 5 erwähnt.

9) THESAURUS OF MUSICAL UNITIES IN SCALE FORM

With the utilization of symmetrical unities in the form of scales, we can free ourselves from pure generative thinking. We can superimpose these scales as well without the pure generation of inversions. Of course the exposition of the entire scale must occur. This insures us of a collection of pitches, irrelevant of the generative process, resulting eventually in a perfect symmetrical unity. Here I have, in letters, an example exhibiting this method. *C-F#-G-Bb* followed by *D-E-A-C*

9) SAMMLUNG MUSIKALISCHER EINHEITEN IN SKALENFORM

Bis jetzt haben wir generierte Spiegelverkehrungen mit einem zentralen Ton aufgebaut. Man könnte auch die gesamten generierten Noten in eine Skala einbauen und diese als Quelle für eine gesamte musikalische Einheit verwenden.

Der Gebrauch musikalischer Einheiten in Skalenform entbindet uns davon, unmäßig viel Energie auf die Erzeugung dieser Strukturen zu verwenden. Wir können die Skalen in gewohnter Weise überlagern, ohne Umkehrungen zu bilden. Natürlich muss die Skala einmal vollständig hörbar vorgestellt werden.

Die Nutzung solcher Skalen sichert die Bildung einer Klangauswahl, die unabhängig von einer reinen Generierung ist und schließlich auch eine vollkommen symmetrische Einheit bildet.

Ein Beispiel für diese Methode: *C-F#-G-B*, gefolgt von *D-E-A-C*.

EXAMPLE 56

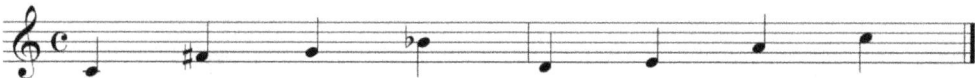

The entire collection is symmetrical to the note D however is not generated from D. This collection is randomly chosen from a symmetrical unity as a heptatonic scale. This reads as such *D-E-F#-G-A-Bb-C*.

Die gesamte Auswahl ist symmetrisch zum Ton D, sie ist aber nicht von D aus generiert worden. Diese Gruppierung ist zufällig ausgewählt von einer symmetrischen Einheit in der Form einer heptatonischen Skale: *D-E-F#-G-A-B-C-D*.

EXAMPLE 57

D as the Central Tone

Therefore we can generate asymmetrical figures or chords with the manifestation of symmetrical scales as resources instead of separate pitches.

A random collection is also possible by rearranging a generated inversion with member substitution. One example could be *D-F-F#-A* followed by a generation *D-B-Bb-G*.

Now we can freely rearrange the perfect generation and construct two random groups that also eventually create a symmetrical unity. For example *B-D-F#-Bb* followed by *G-A-D-F*.

Durch die Niederschrift symmetrischer Skalen haben wir eine Quelle, aus der wir statt einzelner Töne asymmetrische Figuren und Akkorde schöpfen können.

Eine zufällige Zusammenstellung ist auch möglich, indem die Stufen einer erzeugten Umkehrung durch gegenseitiges Vertauschen umarrangiert werden. Als Beispiel: *D-F-F#-A* und die Spiegelverkehrung *D-H-B-G*. Jetzt können wir die in sich stimmige Struktur frei umarrangieren und zwei zufällige Gruppen schaffen, die am Ende ebenso eine symmetrische Einheit ergeben. Eine von vielen Möglichkeiten: *H-D-F#-B* und *G-A-D-F*.

EXAMPLE 58

Now I will illustrate, in Roman numerals, all the possible scales inversely constructed from the beginning pitch.

Es folgt nun in neutralen römischen Ziffern eine Liste aller möglichen Skalen, die in Umkehrung zu ihrem Ausgangston konstruiert sind.

TRITONIC SCALES

I-bII-VII
I-II-bVII
I-bIII-VI
I-III-bVI
I-IV-V

QUADRATONIC SCALES

I-bII-#IV-VII
I-II-#IV-bVII
I-bIII-#IV-VI
I-III-#IV-bVI
I-IV-#IV-V

PENTATONIC SCALES

I-bII-II-#VI-VII
I-bII-bIII-VI-VII
I-bII-III-bVI-VII
I-bII-IV-V-VII
I-II-bIII-VI-bVII
I-II-III-bVI-bVII
I-II-IV-V-bVII
I-#II-III-#V-VI
I-bIII-IV-V-VI
I-III-IV-V-bVI

HEXATONIC SCALES

I-bII-II-#IV-#VI-VII
I-bII-bIII-#IV-VI-VII
I-bII-III-#IV-bVI-VII
I-bII-IV-#IV-V-VII
I-II-bIII-#IV-VI-bVII
I-II-III-#IV-bVI-bVII
I-II-IV-#IV-V-bVII
I-#II-III-#IV-#V-VI
I-bIII-IV-#IV-V-VI
I-III-IV-#IV-V-bVI

HEPTATONIC SCALES

I-bII-II-bIII-VI-bVII-VII
I-bII-II-III-bVI-bVII-VII
I-bII-II-IV-V-bVII-VII
I-bII-bIII-III-bVI-VI-VII
I-bII-bIII-IV-V-VI-VII
I-bII-III-IV-V-bVI-VII
I-II-bIII-III-bVI-VI-bVII
I-II-bIII-IV-V-VI-bVII
I-II-III-IV-V-bVI-bVII
I-#II-III-IV-V-bVI-VI

OCTATONIC SCALES

I-bII-II-bIII-#IV-VI-bVII-VII
I-bII-II-III-#IV-bVI-bVII-VII
I-bII-II-IV-#IV-V-bVII-VII
I-bII-bIII-III-#IV-bVI-VI-VII
I-bII-bIII-IV-#IV-V-VI-VII
I-bII-III-IV-#IV-V-bVI-VII
I-II-bIII-III-#IV-bVI-VI-bVII
I-II-bIII-IV-#IV-V-VI-bVII
I-II-III-IV-#IV-V-bVI-bVII
I-#II-III-IV-#IV-V-bVI-VI

NONETONIC SCALES

I-bII-II-bIII-III-bVI-VI-bVII-VII
I-bII-II-bIII-IV-V-VI-bVII-VII
I-bII-II-III-IV-V-bVI-bVII-VII
I-bII-bIII-III-IV-V-bVI-VI-VII
I-II-bIII-III-IV-V-bVI-VI-bVII

DECATONIC SCALES

I-bII-II-bIII-III-#IV-bVI-VI-bVII-VII
I-bII-II-bIII-IV-#IV-V-VI-bVII-VII
I-bII-II-III-IV-#IV-V-bVI-bVII-VII
I-bII-bIII-III-IV-#IV-V-bVI-VI-VII
I-II-bIII-III-IV-#IV-V-bVI-VI-bVII

UNDECATONIC SCALES

I-bII-II-bIII-III-IV-V-bVI-VI-bVII-VII

9a) MUSICAL UNITIES and SEQUENCES AS SYNTHETIC SYMMETRIES

As we can decipher all musical unities are symmetrical to a given pitch and sequences have an equidistant intervallic symmetry to each tone of a symmetrical axis. Therefore I propose the possibility of utilizing musical unities or various sequences on the tritone or augmented triad as a synthetic symmetry which can bring about the movement of harmony as well. We could pattern a fourth chord or a cluster of three minor seconds as a substitute for a symmetrical axis. In all examples I will superimpose other symmetries.

9a) MUSIKALISCHE EINHEITEN UND SEQUENZEN ALS SYNTHETISCHE SYMMETRIEN

Wie wir sehen können, sind alle musikalischen Einheiten symmetrisch zu einem gegebenen Ton und Sequenzen haben einen gleichmäßigen intervallischen Abstand zu jedem Ton einer symmetrischen Achse. Dafür bietet sich die Möglichkeit, verschiedene Sequenzen als eine synthetische Symmetrie zu verwenden: über den Tritonus, den übermäßigen Dreiklang oder reine musikalische Einheiten. Auch die Bewegung von Harmonien kann so bewältigt werden. Wir können zum Beispiel einen Dreiklang aus Quarten oder ein Cluster von drei kleinen Sekunden als Ersatz für eine symmetrische Achse verwenden. In den folgenden Beispielen werde ich auch andere symmetrische Formen überlagern.

SYNTHETISCHE SYMMETRIE

EXAMPLE 59

Musical unities have a central tone which emerges with a special character which can as a substitute for a symmetrical root, bring about harmonic movement.

The next example employs a larger musical unity with various symmetrical twelve-tone rows in superimposition.

Musikalische Einheiten haben einen Zentralton. Dieser Ton hat einen besonderen Charakter, der als Ersatz für eine symmetrische Wurzel dienen kann.

Das nächste Beispiel nutzt eine größere musikalische Einheit und verschiedene Zwölftonreihen werden überlagert.

116

SYNTHETISCHE SYMMETRIE TEIL 2

EXAMPLE 60

On the other hand as mentioned earlier (see Chapter three page 36) sequences or "partially transposable symmetric modes" have, because of the principle of the "greater intervallic distance", an entire symmetrical axis as a substitution for a symmetrical root.

I will also superimpose various Dorian modes with motivic extension.

(See Chapter 5, Example 33)

Wie vorher erklärt (siehe Kapitel 3, S. 36) kann – wegen des Prinzips des größeren Intervallabstands – eine gesamte symmetrische Achse zusätzlich als Ersatz einer symmetrischen Wurzel verwendet werden. Wir können auch verschiedene dorische Modi mit motivischen Erweiterungen überlagern (siehe Kapitel 5, Beispiel 33).

INTERPOLATION

EXAMPLE 61

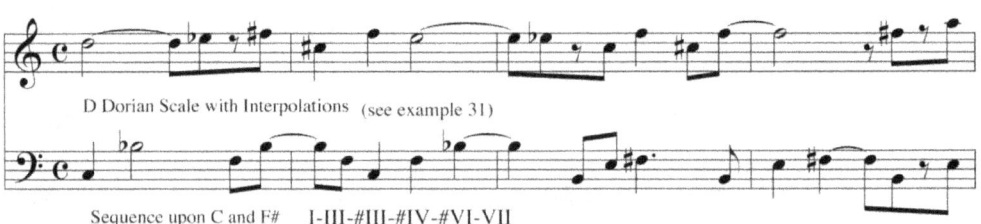

D Dorian Scale with Interpolations (see example 31)

Sequence upon C and F#   I-III-#III-#IV-#VI-VII

Sequence upon A and C# and F   I-#II-III-V-#V-VII

Inversion of the Dorian from G# with interpolation

Sequence on Ab and D   I-#II-III-#III-#IV-VI-#VI-VII

Sequence on E and A#   I-II-III-#III-#IV-#V-#VI-VII   Sequence on G and C#

I-II-III-#III-#IV-#V-#VI-VII   Sequence on F and B   I-II-III-#III-#IV-#V-#VI-VIII

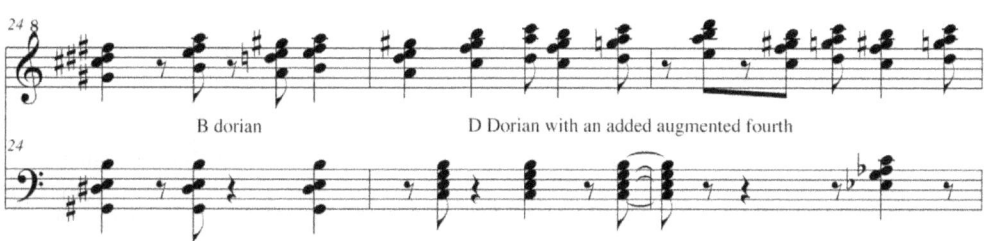

As seen each method can be brought into a logical transposition scheme. Therewith we will receive the movement of harmony however through a variation of the pure tritone or augmented triad in its relationship to the octave. This variation I call a synthetic symmetry which is constructed in equal distance or inversion to an individual note and or its tritone or augmented triad. (see Chapter 11)	Mit jeder Methode lässt sich ein logisches Transpositionsschema erreichen. Harmonische Bewegung erhalten wir durch eine Variation des Tritonus oder übermäßigen Dreiklangs in ihrer Relation zur Oktave. Diese Variation nenne ich eine synthetische Symmetrie, die im gleichen Abstand oder in der Umkehrung eines beliebigen Tons, seines Tritonus oder übermäßigen Dreiklangs konstruiert wird (siehe Kapitel 11).

10) AN ALTERNATIVE METHOD FOR CONTROLLED TRANSPOSITION THROUGH THE USAGE OF ORDERED INVERSIONS AND SYMMETRICAL GENERATION

Firstly I will clarify the definition of a symmetrical generation. This reflects to what I formerly discussed in regards to sequences built upon the tritone or the augmented triad. An Example could be as such. *Ab-C-Eb-G* followed by *C-E-G-B* and *E-G#-B-D#*.

EXAMPLE 62

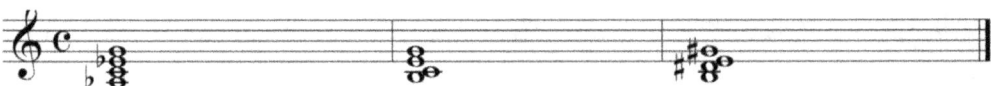

The sequence over the augmented triad can be expanded with modal structures and because of its symmetrical construction it has an inner logic connecting the modal movements. The modes can be freely constructed if the symmetrical matrix stays intact. An example can be *Ab-B-C-D-Eb-E-G* followed by *Db-E-F-G-A-B-C* and finally *C-D#-E-F#-G-Ab-B*. This is what I call symmetrical generation.

EXAMPLE 63

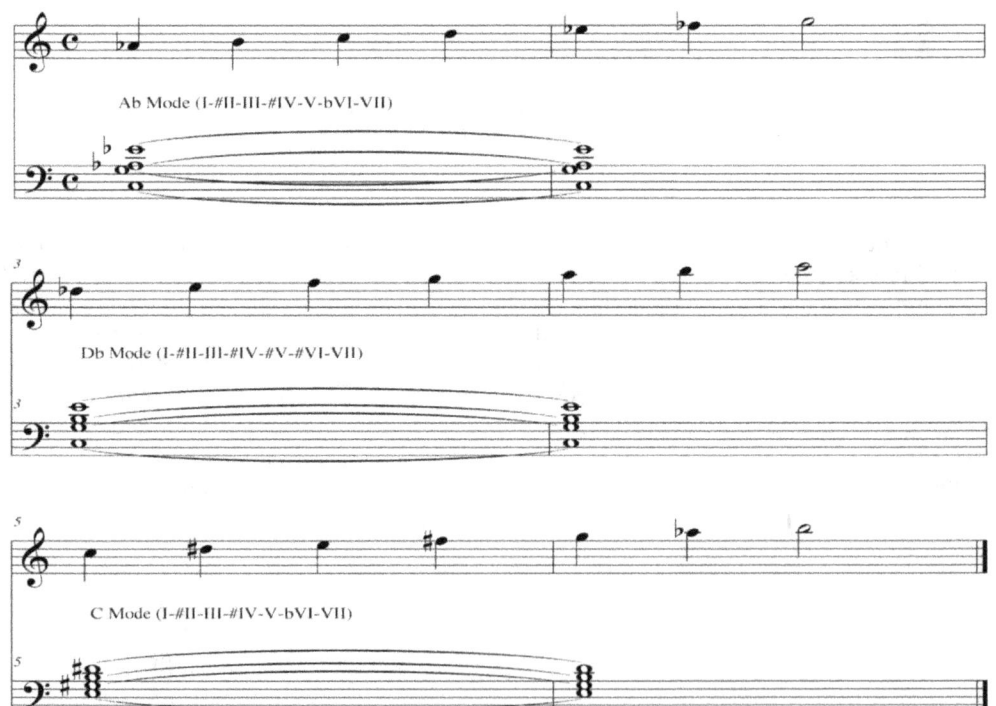

Exactly the same idea can be brought into play with pure inversions or a generation of inversions. This process can also be used as a matrix for modal movement. For example, *C-F-G-Bb* can be followed by *C-G-F-D*, *F-Eb-C-Bb*, *G-E-D-A* and lastly *Bb-Ab-Eb-Db*.

Dieses Verfahren kann auch mit reinen Umkehrungen oder der Generierung von Umkehrungen angewendet werden, die ebenfalls als Matrix für modale Bewegung dienen: *C-F-G-B*, dann *C-G-F-D*, *F-Eb-C-B*, *G-E-D-A* und zuletzt *B-Ab-Eb-Db*.

EXAMPLE 64

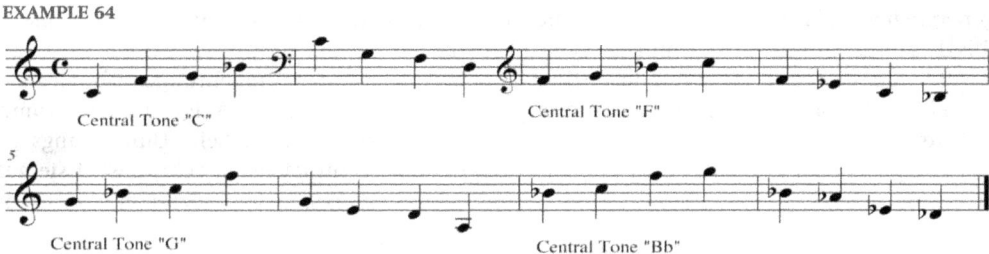

In this example each note is treated as the central point for each inversion. As explained above we can use the ordered inversions as matrixes for controlled transposition. We can generate a succession of modes as such, *C-Eb-F-F#-G-A-Bb-* followed by *D-F-G-G#-A-B-C*, *Gb-A-Bb-C-D-Eb-F*, *A-C-D-D#-E-F#-G* and finally *Fb-G-Ab-Bb-C-Db-Eb*

In diesem Beispiel wird jeder Ton als der Mittelpunkt für die jeweilige Umkehrung behandelt. Wie oben bereits erklärt, können wir die geordnete Umkehrung als Matrix für kontrollierte Transposition nutzen. Wir können eine Abfolge von Modi erzeugen: *C-Eb-F-F#-G-A-B*, *D-F-G-G#-A-H-C*, *Gb-A-B-C-D-Eb-F*, *A-C-D-D#-E-F#-G* und zuletzt *Fb-G-Ab-B-C-Db-Eb*.

EXAMPLE 65

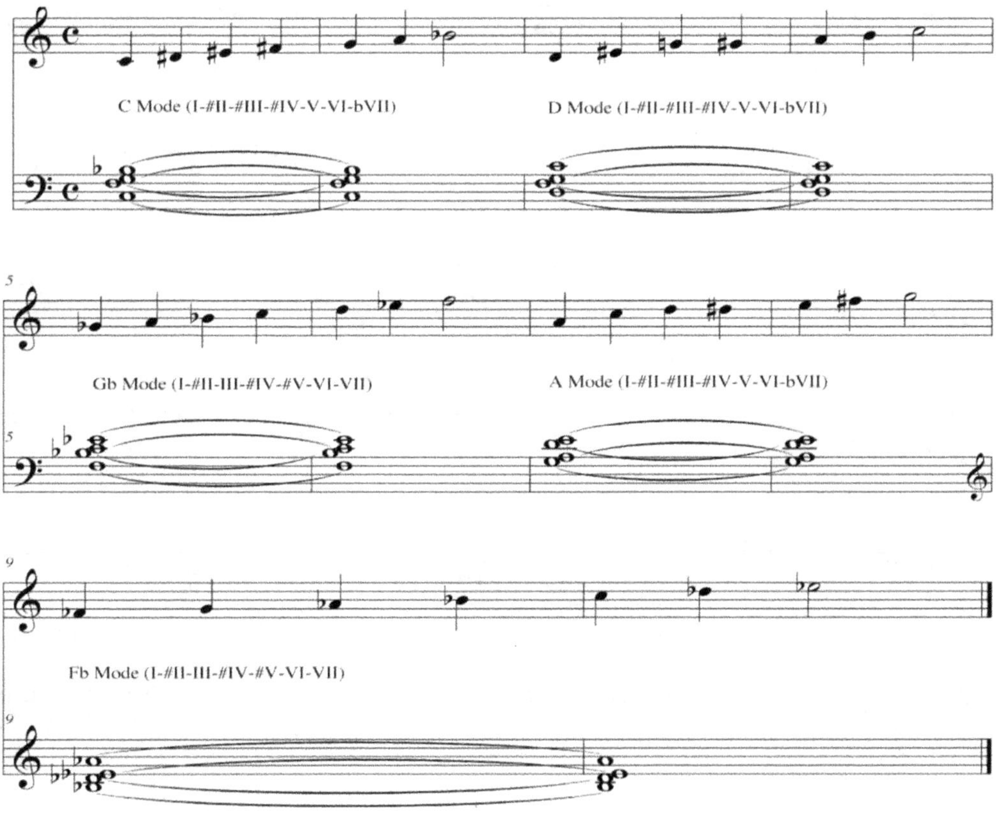

Lastly we can use the entire thesaurus of musical unities as scales, as a matrix for transpositional schemes. One of my favourite methods is to juxtapose chords from given scales that create musical unities and use them as a matrix for the creation of a modal progression. In this example I will generate inversions from each step of a scale from this thesaurus. Because of its symmetrical nature it will be duplicated in inversion. In further generation it will be transposed on various steps of the whole-tone scale.

Man kann alle musikalischen Einheiten, die in der Sammlung aus Kapitel 9 in Skalenform aufgeführt sind, als Matrix für ein Transpositionsschema verwenden. Für meine eigenen Kompositionen bevorzuge ich, Akkorde einer ausgewählten Skala nebeneinander zu setzen, sodass musikalische Einheiten entstehen, die dann wiederum eine Matrix für die modale Progression bilden. Im folgenden Beispiel werden Umkehrungen von jeder Stufe einer Skala gebildet. Aufgrund ihrer symmetrischen Natur wird sie beim Umkehrungsvorgang dupliziert. Im nächsten Schritt wird sie auf verschiedenen Stufen der Ganztonleiter transponiert.

EXAMPLE 66

EXAMPLE 67

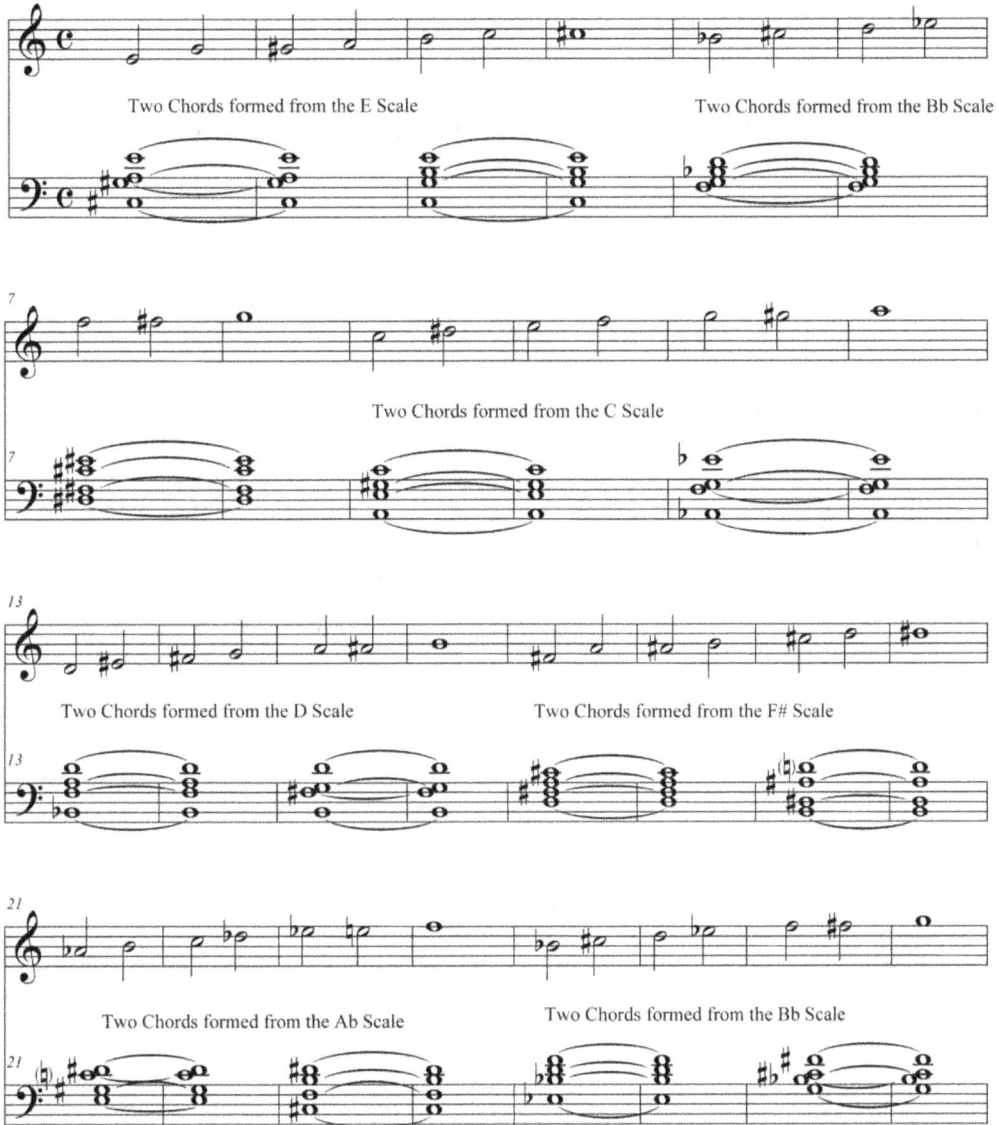

Then we can expand the derivative chords with various modalities.

Schließlich können die aus diesem Vorgang abgeleiteten Akkorde mit verschiedenen Modi erweitert werden.

11) INVERSIONS FROM THE DISTANCE OF A TRITONE AND IN GRADUATING MAJOR THIRDS

Earlier on I discussed a simple sequence upon the tritone and a variation of this sequence. (See Chapter 5) The sequence was *D-Eb-G#-A*. Then I changed the sequence by inverting the intervallic distance from G#. Then the figure appears as such *D-Eb-G#-G*. Because of the intervallic symmetry to a symmetrical axis, such combinations of pitches also can be superimpositions or used as synthetic symmetries.

Now I will expand upon this principle and firstly examine our diatonic mode. Interestingly this mode has the property of the above usage within its entire structure. Looking at an F Lydian we will discover that each intervallic distance from F is equal to the inverted distance from B. A short example could be *F-E-G* and for *B-C-A*.

11) UMKEHRUNGEN DER DISTANZ EINES TRITONUS UND FORTSCHREITENDER GROßER TERZEN

In Kapitel 5 war die Rede von einer simplen Sequenz auf dem Tritonus und einer Variation derselben. Diese Sequenz lautete *D-Eb-G#-A*. Nach Umkehrung der Sequenz auf dem Intervallabstand zu G# erhält man die Variation *D-Eb-G#-G*. Aufgrund der Symmetrie der Intervalle zu einer symmetrischen Achse können solche Tonkombinationen gleichsam Überlagerungen wie auch synthetische Symmetrien sein.

In Erweiterung dieses Prinzips untersuchen wir nun zuerst diesen diatonischen Modus. Interessanterweise harmoniert sein gesamter Aufbau mit der oben beschriebenen Arbeitsweise. Betrachten wir den Modus F Lydisch, werden wir entdecken, dass jede Intervalldistanz zu F gleich der Distanz zu H in der Umkehrung ist. Als kleines Beispiel: *F-E-G* und dazu *H-C-A*.

EXAMPLE 68

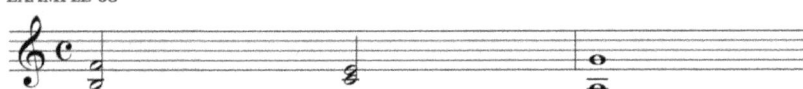

A more expanded figure can be found in this example.

Hier ist ein erweitertes Beispiel.

EXAMPLE 69

Interestingly there are few scales in music with this special property. I will now bring one of the non-diatonic modes into play.

Es gibt wenige Skalen in der Musik mit dieser Eigenschaft. Hier ist eine Figur von einem nicht-diatonischen Modus:

EXAMPLE 70

These modes I will construct so that a starting point is visible and therefore the usage of the scale is twofold. Either we have the possibility to apply the structures as unequally distributed modes or as sequences upon symmetrical axes. I will now present a thesaurus of these modal structures.

Es folgt nun eine Sammlung solcher modalen Konstrukte, wieder in römischen Ziffern mit sichtbarem Grundton. Dafür gibt es einen zweifachen Gebrauch solcher Modi.

Entweder kann man sie als ungleich verteilte Modi oder als Umkehrungen zu einer Symmetrieachse betrachten.

A. INVERSIONS FROM THE TRITONE
   and AUGMENTED TRIAD AS SCALES

1. I-#IV-VI
2. I-#IV-V-VII
3. I-#IV-#V-bVII
4. I-#IV-V-VI-VII
5. I-#IV-#V-VI-bVII
6. I-bIII-#IV-V-VII
7. I-bIII-#IV-#V-bVII
8. I-#IV-V-bIV-#VI-VII
9. I-bII-IV-#IV-V-VII
10. I-II-III-#IV-V-VII
11. I-bIII-#IV-V-VI-VII
12. I-bIII-#IV-#V-VI-bVII
13. I-bII-IV-#IV-V-VI-VII
14. I-bII-IV-#IV-#V-VI-bVII
15. I-II-III-#IV-V-VI-VII
16. I-II-III-#IV-#V-VI-bVII
17. I-bIII-#IV-V-bVI-#VI-VII
18. I-bIII-#IV-V-bVI-VI-#VI-VII
19. I-bII-IV-#IV-V-bVI-#VI-VII
20. I-II-III-#IV-V-bVI-#VI-VII
21. I-bII-II-III-IV-#IV-V-bVI-#VI-VII
22. I-bII-bIII-IV-#IV-V-bVI-#VI-VII
23. I-II-bIII-III-#IV-V-bVI-#VI-VII
24. I-bII-IV-#IV-V-bVI-VI-#VI-VII
25. I-II-III-#IV-V-bVI-VI-#VI-VII
26. I-bII-bIII-IV-#IV-V-bVI-VI-#VI-VII
27. I-bII-II-III-IV-#IV-V-#V-#VI-VII
28. I-II-bIII-III-#IV-V-bVI-VI-#VI-VII

A. INVERSIONS FROM THE MAJOR THIRD
   OF THE AUGMENTED TRIAD

In these cases I will visually assist the understanding
of the inversion and then construct each scale
with a starting point as Roman numeral "I".
Each starting point is emphasized with a black marking.

1. I-bII-**III**-#II-#V-VI (I-III-IV-#V-VI-VII)
2. I-II-**III**-II-#V-#VI (I-III-#IV-#V-bVII)
3. I-#II-III-bII-**#V**-VII (I-III-V-#V-VI-VII)
4. I-IV-III-VII-**#V**-bII (I-#II-III-IV-#V-VI)
5. I-#IV-III-#VI-#V-II (whole tone scale)
6. I-V-**III**-VI-#V-#II (I-#II-III-IV-#V-VII)
7. I-VI-III-V-#V-IV (I-III-IV-V-#V-VI)
8. I-bVII-III-#IV-#V-#IV (I-III-#IV-#V-bVII)
9. **I**-VII-III-IV-#V-V (I-III-IV-V-#V-VII)
10. I-bII-II-**III**-#II-II-#V-VI-bVII (I-III-IV-#IV-#V-VI-#VI-VII)
11. I-bII-#II-**III**-#II-bII-#V-VI-VII (I-III-IV-V-#V-VI-VII)
12. I-bII-III-**III**-#II-I-#V-VI-I (I-III-IV-#V-VI-VII)
13. I-bII-IV-**III**-#II-VII-#V-VI-bII (I-bII-III-IV-V-#V-VI-VII)
14. I-bII-#IV-**III**-#II-#VI-#V-VI-II (I-II-III-IV-#IV-#V-VI-#VI-VII)
15. I-bII-V-**III**-#II-VI-#V-VI-#II (I-#II-III-IV-#V-VI-VII)
16. I-bII-bVI-**III**-#II-bVI-#V-VI-III (I-III-IV-#V-VI-VII)
17. I-bII-VI-III-#II-V-**#V**-VI-IV (I-bII-III-IV-#V-VI-VII)
18. I-bII-bVII-**III**-#II-#IV-#V-VI-#IV (I-II-III-IV-#IV-#V-VI-VII)
19. **I**-bII-VII-**III**-#II-IV-**#V**-VI-V (I-bII-#II-III-IV-#V-VI-VII)
20. I-II-#II-**III**-II-bII-#V-#VI-VII (I-III-IV-V-#V-VI-#VI-VII)
21. I-II-III-**III**-II-I-#V-bVII-I (I-III-#IV-#V-bVII)
22. I-II-IV-III-II-VII-#V-bVII-bII (I-bII-III-#IV-V-#V-VI-bVII)
23. I-II-#IV-III-II-bVII-#V-#VI-II (whole tone scale)
24. I-II-V-**III**-II-VI-#V-bVII-#II (I-#II-III-#IV-#V-VI-VII)
25. I-II-bVI-**III**-II-bVI-#V-#VI-III (I-III-#IV-V#-bVII)
26. **I**-II-VI-III-II-V-#V-#VI-IV (I-II-III-IV-#V-#V-VI-bVII)
27. I-II-bVII-III-II-#IV-#V-#VII-#IV (whole tone scale)
28. I-II-VII-III-II-IV-#V-#VI-V (I-II-III-IV-V-#V-#VI-VII)

29. I-bIII-III-**III**-bII-I-#V-VII-I (I-III-V-#V-VI-VII)
30. I-bIII-IV-**III**-bII-VII-#V-VII-bII (I-bII-III-V-#V-VI-VII)
31. I-bIII-#IV-**III**-bII-bVII-#V-VII-II (I-II-III-#IV-V-#V-#VI-VII)
32. I-bIII-V-**III**-bII-VI-#V-VII-#II (I-#II-III-IV-V-#V-VI-VII)
33. I-bIII-bVI-**III**-bII-bVI-#V-VII-III (I-III-V-#V-VII)
34. **I**-bIII-VI-**III**-bII-V-**#V**-VII-IV (I-bII-#II-III-IV-V-#V-VI-VII)
35. I-bIII-bVII-**III**-bII-#IV-#V-VII-#IV (I-II-III-#IV-V-#V-VI-VII)
36. I-bIII-VII-III-bII-IV-**#V**-VII-V (I-#II-III-IV-V-#V-VI-VII)
37. I-III-IV-III-I-VIII-**#V**-I-bII (I-#II-III-IV-#V-VI)
38. I-III-#IV-III-I-bVII-#V-I-II (whole tone scale)
39. I-III-V-III-I-VI-#V-I-#II (I-#II-III-IV-#V-VII)
40. I-III-VI-III-I-V-#V-I-IV (I-III-IV-V-#V-VI)
41. I-III-bVII-III-I-#IV-#V-I-#IV (I-III-#IV-#V-bVII)
42. I-III-VII-III-I-IV-#V-I-V (I-III-IV-V-#V-VII)
43. I-IV-#IV-III-VII-#VI-**#V**-bII-II (I-II-#II-III-IV-#IV-#V-VI-bVII)
44. **I**-IV-V-**III**-VII-VI-**#V**-bII-bIII (I-bII-#II-III-IV-#V-VI-VII)
45. I-IV-bVI-III-VII-#V-**#V**-bII-III (I-#II-III-IV-#V-VI)
46. I-IV-VI-III-VII-V-#V-bII-IV (I-bII-III-IV-V-#V-VI-VII)
47. **I**-IV-bVII-III-VII-#IV-#V-bII-#IV (I-bII-III-IV-#IV-#V-VI-VII)
48. I-IV-VII-III-VII-IV-**#V**-bII-V (I-#II-III-IV-V-#V-VI-VII)
49. I-#IV-V-**III**-#VI-VI-#V-II-#II (I-II-#II-III-IV-#IV-#V-#VI-VII)
50. I-#IV-bVI-III-#VI-#V-#V-II-III (whole tone scale)
51. I-#IV-VI-III-#VI-V-#V-II-IV (I-II-III-IV-#IV-V-#V-VI-bVII)
52. I-#IV-bVII-III-#VI-#IV-#V-II-#IV (whole tone scale)
53. I-#IV-VII-III-#VI-IV-#V-II-V (I-II-III-IV-#IV-V-#V-#VI-VII)
54. I-V-bVI-**III**-VI-#V-#V-#II-III (I-#II-III-IV-#V-VII)
55. I-V-VI-III-VI-V-**#V**-#II-IV (I-bII-III-V-#V-VI-VII)
56. **I**-V-bVII-III-VI-#IV-#V-#II-#IV (I-#II-III-#IV-V-#V-VI-bVII)
57. I-V-VII-III-VI-IV-#V-#II-V (I-#II-III-IV-#V-VI-VII)
58. I-bVI-VII-III-bVI-V-#V-III-V (I-III-IV-V-#V-VI)
59. I-bVI-bVII-III-bVI-#IV-#V-III-#IV (I-III-#IV-#V-bVII)
60. I-bVI-VII-III-bVI-IV-#V-III-V (I-III-IV-V-#V-VII)
61. I-VI-bVII-III-V-#IV-#V-IV-#IV (I-III-IV-#IV-V-#V-VI-bVII)
62. I-VI-VII-III-V-IV-#V-IV-V (I-III-IV-V-#V-VI-VII)
63. I-#VI-VII-III-#IV-IV-#V-IV-V (I-III-IV-#IV-V-#V-#VI-VII)

B. INVERSIONS FROM THE MAJOR THIRD and the AUGMENTED FIFTH OF THE AUGMENTED TRIADS

1. I-bII-III-#II-**#V**-V (I-III-IV-V-#V-VII)
2. I-II-**III**-II-#V-#IV (I-III-#IV-#V-bVII)
3. I-#II-III-bII-**#V**-IV (I-III-IV-V-#V-VI)
4. I-IV-III-VII-#V-#II (I-#II-III-IV-#V-VII)
5. I-#IV-III-#VI-#V-II (whole tone scale)
6. I-V-**III**-VI-#V-bII (I-#II-III-IV-#V-VI)
7. I-VI-III-V-#V-VII (I-III-V-#V-VI-VII)
8. I-bVII-III-#IV-#V-bVII(I-III-#IV-#V-bVII)
9. **I**-VII-III-IV-#V-VI (I-III-IV-#V-VI-VII)
10. I-bII-II-III-#II-II-**#V**-V-#IV (I-III-IV-#IV-V-#V-#VI-VII)
11. I-bII-#II-III-#II-bII-**#V**-V-IV (I-III-IV-V-#V-VI-VII)
12. I-bII-III-III-#II-I-**#V**-V-III (I-III-IV-V-#V-VII)
13. I-bII-IV-III-#II-VII-**#V**-V-#II (I-#II-III-IV-#V-VI-VII)
14. I-bII-#IV-III-#II-#VI-**#V**-V-II (I-II-III-IV-#IV-V-#V-#VI-VII)
15. I-bII-V-**III**-#II-VI-#V-V-bII (I-#II-III-IV-#V-VI)
16. I-bII-bVI-III-#II-bVI-**#V**-V-I (I-III-IV-V-#V-VII)
17. I-bII-**III**-#II-V-#V-V-VII (I-#II-III-IV-#V-VI-VII)
18. I-bII-bVII-III-#II-#IV-**#V**-V-bVII (I-II-III-IV-#V-#V-#VI-VII)
19. **I**-bII-VII-**III**-#II-IV-**#V**-V-VI (I-bII-#II-III-IV-V-#V-#VI-VII)
20. I-II-#II-III-II-bII-**#V**-#IV-IV (I-III-#IV-V-#V-VI-bVII)
21. I-II-III-**III**-II-I-#V-#IV-III (I-III-#IV-#V-bVII)
22. I-II-IV-III-II-VII-**#V**-#IV-#II (I-#II-III-IV-#V-VI-bVII)
23. I-II-#IV-III-II-bVII-#V-#IV-II (whole tone scale)
24. I-II-V-III-II-VI-**#V**-#IV-bII (I-bII-III-IV-#IV-#V-#VI-VII)
25. I-II-bVI-III-II-bVI-**#V**-#IV-I (I-III-#IV-#V-bVII)
26. I-II-VI-III-II-V-#V-#IV-VII (I-II-III-#IV-V-#V-VI-VII)

127

27. I-II-bVII-III-II-#IV-#V-#IV-bVII (whole tone scale)
28. I-II-VII-III-II-IV-#V-#IV-VI (I-II-III-IV-#IV-#V-VI-VII)
29. I-bIII-III-III-bII-I-**#V**-IV-III (I-III-IV-V-#V-VI)
30. I-bIII-IV-**III**-bII-VII-#V-IV-#II (I-bII-III-V-#V-VI-VII)
31. I-bIII-#IV-III-bII-bVII-**#V**-IV-II (I-II-III-IV-#IV-V-#V-VI-bVII)
32. I-bIII-V-III-bII-VI-**#V**-IV-bII (I-bII-III-IV-V-#V-VI-VII)
33. I-bIII-bVI-III-bII-bVI-**#V**-IV-I (I-III-IV-V-#V-VI)
34. I-bIII-VI-**III**-bII-V-**#V**-IV-VII (I-bII-#II-III-IV-V-#V-VI-VII)
35. I-bIII-bVII-III-bII-#IV-**#V**-IV-bVII (I-II-III-IV-V-#V-VI-bVII)
36. I-bIII-VII-**III**-bII-IV-#V-IV-VI (I-bII-III-IV-#V-VI-VII)
37. I-III-IV-III-I-VII-#V-III-#II (I-#II-III-IV-#V-VII)
38. I-III-#IV-III-I-bVII-#V-III-II (whole tone scale)
39. I-III-V-**III**-I-VI-#V-III-bII (I-#II-III-IV-#V-VI)
40. I-III-VI-III-I-V-#V-III-VII (I-III-V-#V-VI-VII)
41. **I**-III-bVII-III-I-#IV-#V-III-bVII (I-III-#IV-#V-bVII)
42. I-III-VII-III-I-IV-#V-III-VI (I-III-IV-#V-VI-VII)
43. I-IV-#IV-III-VII-#VI-#V-#II-II (I-II-#II-III-IV-#IV-#V-VI-VII)
44. I-IV-V-**III**-VII-VI-**#V**-#II-bII (I-bII-#II-III-IV-V-#V-VI-VII)
45. I-IV-bVI-III-VII-bVI-#V-#II-I (I-#II-III-IV-#V-VII)
46. I-IV-VI-III-VII-V-#V-#II-VII (I-#II-III-V-#V-VI-VII)
47. I-IV-bVII-III-VII-#IV-#V-#II-bVII (I-#II-III-IV-#IV-#V-#VI-VII)
48. I-IV-VII-III-VII-IV-#V-#II-VI (I-#II-III-IV-#V-VI-VII)
49. I-#IV-V-**III**-#VI-VI-#V-II-bII (I-II-#II-III-IV-#IV-#V-VI-bVII)
50. I-#IV-bVI-III-#VI-bVI-#V-II-I (whole tone scale)
51. I-#IV-VI-III-#VI-V-#V-II-VII (I-II-III-#IV-V-#V-#VI-VII)
52. I-#IV-bVII-III-#VI-#IV-#V-II-bVII (whole tone scale)
53. **I**-#IV-VII-III-#VI-IV-#V-II-VI (I-II-III-IV-#IV-V-#V-VI-#VI-VII)
54. I-V-bVI-**III**-VI-bVI-#V-bII-I (I-#II-III-IV-#V-VI)
55. I-V-VI-III-VI-V-#V-bII-VII (I-bII-III-V-#V-VI-VII)
56. I-V-bVII-III-VI-#IV-#V-bII-bVII(I-bII-III-#IV-#V-VI-bVII)
57. I-V-VII-III-VI-IV-#V-bII-VI (I-bII-III-IV-#V-VI-VII)
58. I-bVI-VI-III-bVI-V-#V-I-VII (I-III-V-#V-VI-VII)
59. I-bVI-bVII-III-bVI-#IV-#V-I-bVII (I-III-#IV-bVI-bVII)
60. I-bVI-VII-III-bVI-V-#V-I-VI (I-III-V-#V-VI-VII)
61. I-VI-bVII-III-V-#IV-#V-VII-bVII (I-III-#IV-V-#V-VI-#VI-VII)
62. I-VI-VII-III-V-IV-#V-VII-VI (I-III-IV-V-#V-VI-VII)
63. I-#VI-VII-III-#IV-IV-#V-bVII-VI (I-III-IV-#IV-#V-VI-bVII)

Of course we are always, within this technique, free of modal structures and can develop melodic figures based on the principle of inversions upon the axes of symmetries. In the realm of melodic figures our horizons are endless. A few examples can be found at the beginning of chapter five. Here I will exemplify other such figures.

Bei dieser Technik müssen wir uns nicht vom Korsett modaler Strukturen einengen lassen, wir können unsere Melodiefiguren mit Hilfe des Umkehrungsprinzips auf den symmetrischen Achsen entwickeln. Im Reich der melodischen Gestaltung gibt es keinen einengenden Horizont!

Ein paar Beispiele finden sich am Beginn von Kapitel 5. Weitere Figuren dieser Art sind hier abgebildet:

EXAMPLE 71

We can as well develop related inversions by moving the beginning point of each inversion.

Miteinander verwandte Umkehrungen können durch Bewegen ihres Ausgangspunktes entwickelt werden:

EXAMPLE 72

[Musical notation: measures 1-20 with annotations "F-B inverted to one another", "G and C# inverted to one another", "Bb-E inverted to one another", "F# and C inverted to one another", "G and C# inverted to one another"]

We can independently once again use the generated scales as transposable unequally distributed modes and superimpose the same structures as musical unites.

In unserer Arbeitsweise völlig frei und unabhängig können wir die erzeugten Skalen einmal mehr als transponierbare ungleichmäßig verteilte Modi nutzen und dieselben Strukturen als musikalische Einheiten überlagern.

ÜBERMÄßIG

EXAMPLE 73

Inversion from the mode in bass starting on "C" with generations of inversions producing the original mode

C Mode (I-#II-III-IV-V-#V-VI-VII)

Ab Mode (I-bII-III-IV-V-#V-VI-VII)

Mode C-Db-E-F-G-Ab-A-B see Scale 15 from
Inversion from the Major Third of an Augmented Triad

Mode Ab-B-C-Db-Eb-E-F-G see scale 25
Inversion from the Major Third of an Augmented Triad

D Mode (I-bII-III-IV-V-#V-VI-VII)

Mode Bb-C#-D-Eb-F-F#-G-A see scale 25
Inversion from the Major Third of an Augmented Triad

E Mode (I-bII-III-IV-V-#V-VI-VII)

Ped.
Mode E-G-G#-A-B-C-C#-D# see scale 25
Inversion from the Major Third of an Augmented Triad

Gb Mode (I-bII-III-IV-V-#V-VI-VII)   Bb Mode (I-bII-III-IV-V-#V-VI-VII) C Mode (I-bII-III-IV-V-#V-VI-VII)

Mode F#-A-A#-B-C#-D-D#-E# see scale 25   Ped.
Inversion from the Major Third of an Augmented Triad   Mode Bb-C#-D-Eb-F-F#-G-A see scale 25
Inversion from the Major Third of an Augmented Triad

D Mode (I-bII-III-IV-V-#V-VI-VII)

Mode C-D#-E-F-G-G#-A-B see scale 25
Inversion from the Major Third of an Augmented Triad

There also exist other variants that we can employ. One variant could be the addition of a tone to a particular symmetrical axis that is also symmetrical through inversion. An example could be as such. *C-Db-F-F#-G* or perhaps *C-Db-D#-E-F-G-G#-A*.

Außerdem gibt es weitere anwendbare Varianten. Eine Variante besteht darin, einen zusätzlichen Ton zu der symmetrischen Achse hinzuzufügen. Durch Umkehren wird dieser zu einer Stufe dieser Achse. Ein Beispiel ist *C-Des-F-Fis-G* oder vielleicht *C-Des-Dies-E-F-G-Gis-A*.

EXAMPLE 73a

Another example could be a sequence over a symmetrical axis, for example, the augmented triad and a superimposition of the other symmetrical

Eine andere Variante ist die Generierung über eine symmetrische Achse, z.B. der übermäßige Dreiklang mit Überlagerung der anderen Achse,

axis, the tritone. An example could be *Gb-G-A-Bb-C-D-Eb-Gb*.

EXAMPLE 73b

To understand this we shall extract the symmetrical axis (*Gb-Bb-D*). Each point of the axis receives a half step either above or below itself. Then, as proposed, we can superimpose the tritone (*Gb-C*). When we enharmonically change *Gb to F#* we can witness that this example is actually the harmonic minor scale of traditional tonality. In fact the other two commonly used scales of tonal music were the diatonic and the ascending minor scale. The diatonic is of course full of symmetrical qualities especially through the usage of the Dorian mode. The ascending melodic minor scale, when played from the fifth step is also a musical unity.

12) CONTROLLING THE DYNAMICS OF TRANSPOSITION THROUGH THE NATURE OF THE OVERTONE SERIES

Through my work with this concept I once discovered a fascinating phenomenon involving the movement of various modal transpositions. For example a mode with the starting point "C" has eleven possible destinations. Each of these eleven steps will eventually be found in our natural overtone series.

I propose that each movement has a certain dramatic effect dependent on the distance the movement is up the overtone series. For example a movement from a mode with a starting point "C" will lilt lightly to a mode with a "G" starting point. "G" is of course, as the perfect fifth from "C", the next overtone after the octave and the first transposition in the gradation of overtones.

The entire gradation as each chromatic appears reads as follows:

1st. The perfect fifth	1. Die reine Quinte
2nd. The major third	2. Die große Terz
3rd. The minor seventh	3. Die kleine Septime
4th. The major second	4. Die große Sekunde
5th. The augmented fourth	5. Die übermäßige Quarte
6th. The major sixth	6. Die große Sexte
7th. The major seventh	7. Die große Septime
8th. The minor second	8. Die kleine Sekunde
9th. The minor third	9. Die kleine Terz
10th. The perfect fourth	10. Die reine Quarte
11th. The minor sixth.	11. Die kleine Sexte

EXAMPLE 74

In this example I used modes with only one symmetrical axis however the same effect is also audible with modes with multiple symmetrical axes.

Im obigen Beispiel finden nur Modi mit einer Symmetrieachse Anwendung. Der Effekt ist natürlich auch hörbar bei Modi mit mehreren Symmetrieachsen.

EXAMPLE 75

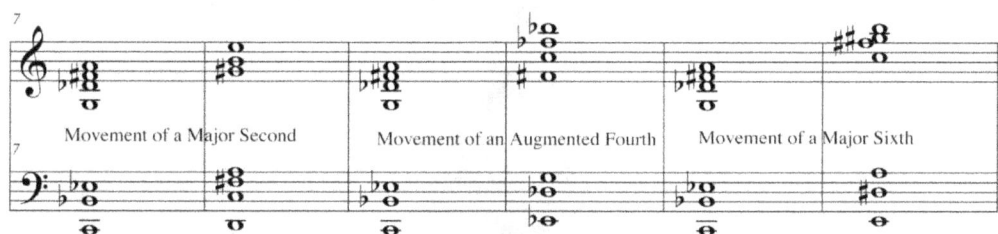

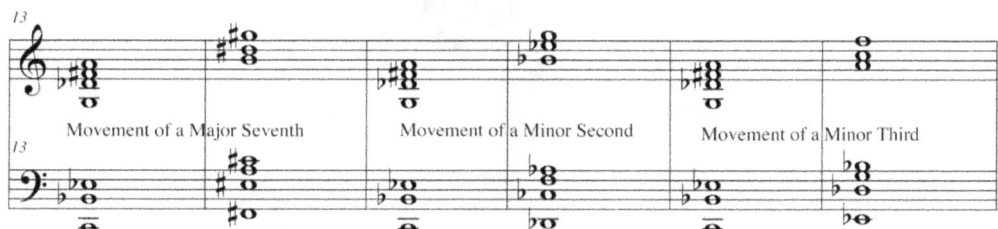

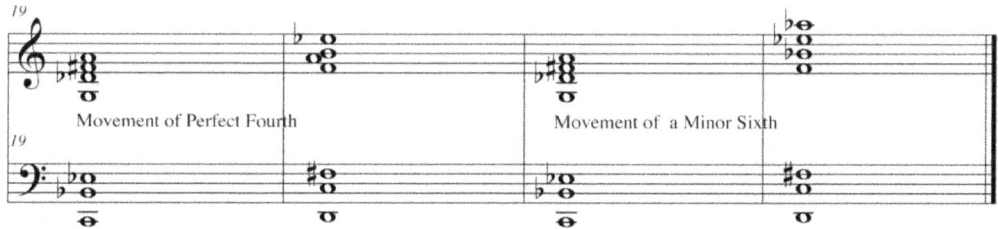

As we know some overtones are approximate because their intonation is slightly outside a well-tempered environment. However within the well-tempered environment these relationships come to fruition.

As the movement from a "C" starting point to a "G" starting point is very light exactly the opposite occurs with a movement from a "C" starting point to an "Ab" starting point.

Natürlich kann man sich auf diese Weise den Obertönen nur annähern, denn sie entsprechen bekanntlich nicht den Tönen der temperierten Stimmung. Die sich aus der Obertonreihe ergebenden Zusammenhänge kommen jedoch auch innerhalb der Temperierung zur Geltung.

So wie die Bewegung vom Ausgangspunkt C zum G sehr leicht klingt, so geschieht das genaue Gegenteil mit einer Bewegung vom Ausgangspunkt C zum Ab.

This is a very dramatic modulation. As presented a modal movement increases in dramatic effect the further the intervallic distance is up the overtones series. So in letters with a "C" starting point it would look like this. "C" to "G" is a light movement and with each following the modulation increases in intensity. We could, as well, describe it in colours from the spectrum yellow to ultra violet.

Dies ist eine sehr dramatische Modulation. Dieser dramatische Effekt einer modalen Bewegung erhöht sich, je weiter der Zielton in der Obertonreihe vom Grundton entfernt ist. C nach G ist eine sanfte Bewegung, mit jeder folgenden legt die Modulation an Intensität zu. Wir könnten dies auch als Farbtöne ausdrücken – von gelb bis ultraviolett.

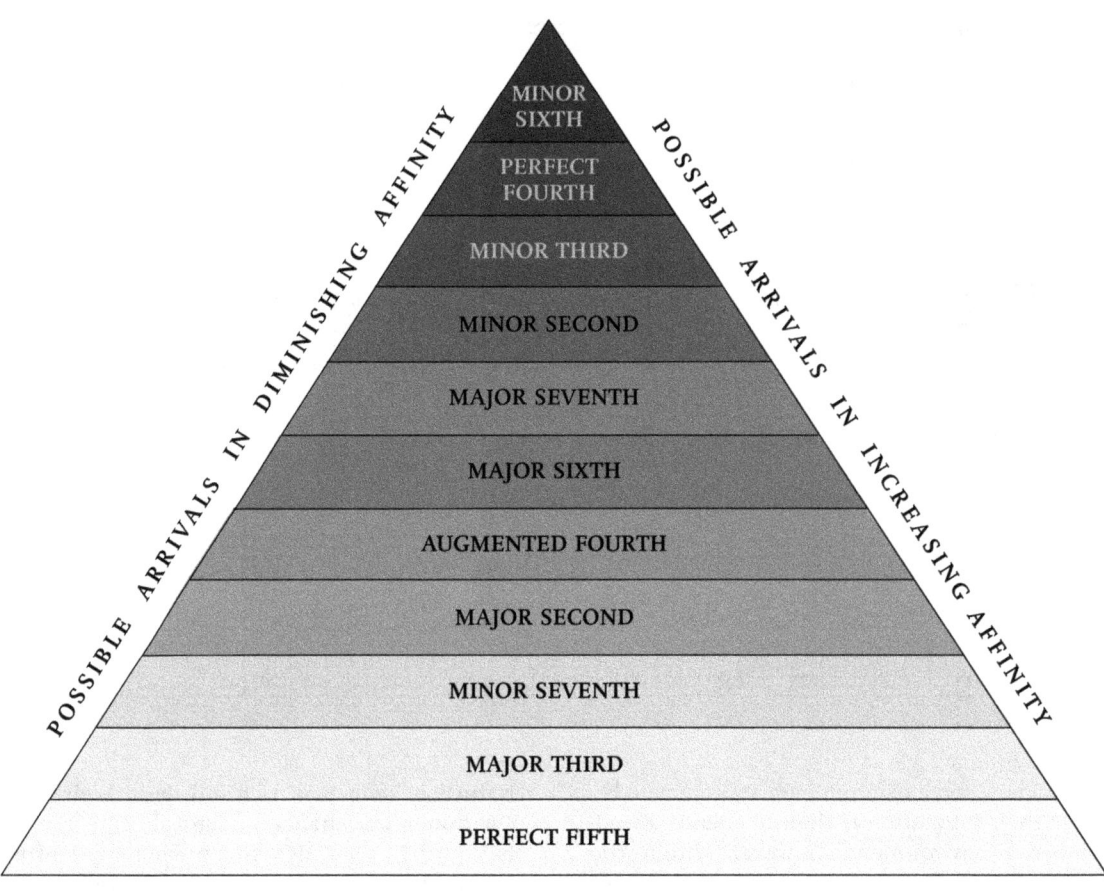

I will now construct a small piece with each movement becoming more intense and then returning to the least intense.

Zur Veranschaulichung folgt eine kleine Komposition.

AFFINITÄTEN

EXAMPLE 77

The application of this technique is in no fashion a prerequisite or the only method possible for dramatic control in music however it is a useful tool when consciously practiced.

Diese Technik ist keineswegs Voraussetzung oder die einzig mögliche Methode für die Kontrolle der Dramatik in der Musik. Sie ist jedoch ein sehr nützliches Werkzeug, wenn sie bewusst eingesetzt wird.

13) THE POLYMODAL MARRIAGE OF AN ORDERED INVERTED ENVIRONMENT

Through the concept of inverted figures upon each given member of a chord, this technique can of course be utilized as well with a chosen modality. For example we could choose any mode presented in my thesaurus and initialize a generation of ordered inversions.

Firstly I will now construct a heptatonic mode *C-Db-E-F#-G-Ab-Bb*. Then as discussed earlier I will generate inversions in relation to each separate note of the existing mode.

We will then generate a row of seven modes related to the original. This generation can create a string of related melodic patterns that can be polymodally superimposed upon the same exact generation in another register. If the two modal environments retain identity they will function as a transpositional scheme or as a superimposition. The superimposition is of course possible to transpose and can begin from another pitch but will still obtain the original pitch relationships.

Therefore I could develop the original inverted scheme and then we could simultaneously superimpose the sevenfold collection in the retrograde beginning on perhaps Ab where the original would begin with C.

From the original mode I will now demonstrate our seven inversions.

Firstly from "C" *C-B-Ab-F#-F-E-D*

Secondly we have "Db" - resulting in *Db-Bb-Ab-G-F#-E-D*.

Thirdly then from "E"-resulting in *E-D-C#-C-Bb-Ab-G*.

Fourthly from "F#"- resulting in *F#-F-E-D-C-B-G#*..

Fifthly we invert from "G" bringing about *G-F#-E-D-C#-Bb-Ab*.

Sixthly from "Ab"and this results in *Ab-Gb-E-Eb-C-Bb-A* and

seventh and lastly the inversion from "Bb" appears as the following *Bb-Ab-G-E-D-C#-C*.

13) POLYMODALITÄT UND DIE GEORDNETE UMKEHRUNGSUMGEBUNG

Die Technik der musikalischen Gestaltschöpfung durch Umkehrung auf jedem Teilton eines Akkordes kann natürlich auch auf einen frei wählbaren Modus angewendet werden. Wir können jeden beliebigen Modus aus der in diesem Buch präsentierten Sammlung auswählen und mit der Erzeugung geordneter Umkehrungen beginnen.

Exemplarisch hier ein heptatonischer Modus: *C-Db-E-F#-G-Ab-B*. Wir erzeugen nun Umkehrungen in Bezug zu jedem einzelnen Ton des Modus.

Auf diese Weise erhalten wir sieben Modi, die mit den ursprünglichen verwandt sind. Dieser Vorgang kann eine Kette verwandter Melodiepatterns hervorbringen, die, in einem separaten Verzeichnis, exakt den gleichen zuvor erzeugten Modi polymodal überlagert werden können. Solange die beiden nun vorhandenen modalen Umgebungen ihre Identität bewahren, werden sie als ein Transpositionsschema oder als Überlagerung funktionieren. Die Überlagerung ist freilich transponierbar und kann einen beliebigen Ausgangston besitzen, doch die Intervallbeziehungen bleiben bestehen.

Wie bereits erwähnt, kann man ein originales Umkehrungsschema entwickeln und gleichzeitig die Gruppe der sieben erzeugten Modi im Umkehrschluss überlagern. Als Ausgangston eignet sich zum Beispiel As, wenn der Ursprungsmodus mit C begann.

Ausgehend vom originalen Modus *C-Db-E-F#-G-Ab-B* demonstriere ich nun die sieben Umkehrungen:

1. von C   => *C-H-Ab-F#-F-E-D*
2. von Db => *Db-B-Ab-G-F#-E-D*
3. von E   => *E-D-C#-C-B-Ab-G*
4. von F# => *F#-F-E-D-C-H-G#*
5. von G   => *G-F#-E-D-C#-B-Ab*
6. von Ab => *Ab-Gb-Fb-Eb-C-B-A*
7. von Bb => *B-Ab-G-E-D-C#-C*

EXAMPLE 78

Central Tone "C"

Central Tone "Db"

Central Tone "E"

Central Tone "F#"

Central Tone "G"

Central Tone "Ab"

Central Tone "Bb"

Rearranging the notes one will find that we have generated the same mode in varying transpositions all landing on the matrix of the whole-tone gradation. This can exquisitely become our transpositional scheme.

Wenn man die Töne umarrangiert, wird man erkennen, dass der gleiche Modus in unterschiedlichen Transpositionen erzeugt wurde. Dabei stimmen sie alle mit der Matrix der Ganztonleiter überein. Dies kann auf hervorragende Weise als Transpositionsschema dienen.

EXAMPLE 79

Original Mode — Generated Mode #1 — Generated Mode #2

Generated Mode #3 — Generated Mode #4 — Generated Mode #5

Generated Mode #6 — Generated Mode #7

In this way we develop transposed modes as well as possible superimpositions that all use the same generative process. We can then take the generated mode and develop seven inversions resulting in the original mode as well found in various transpositions on the matrix of the whole-tone gradation.

Auf diese Weise entwickelt man transponierte Modi zusammen mit möglichen Überlagerungen in ein und demselben Prozess.

In einem weiteren Schritt können aus einem durch Umkehrung erzeugten Modus sieben weitere Umkehrungen entstehen, was u.a. den Ursprungsmodus zum Ergebnis hat, der in verschiedenen Transpositionen auf der Matrix der Ganztonskala wiedergefunden werden kann.

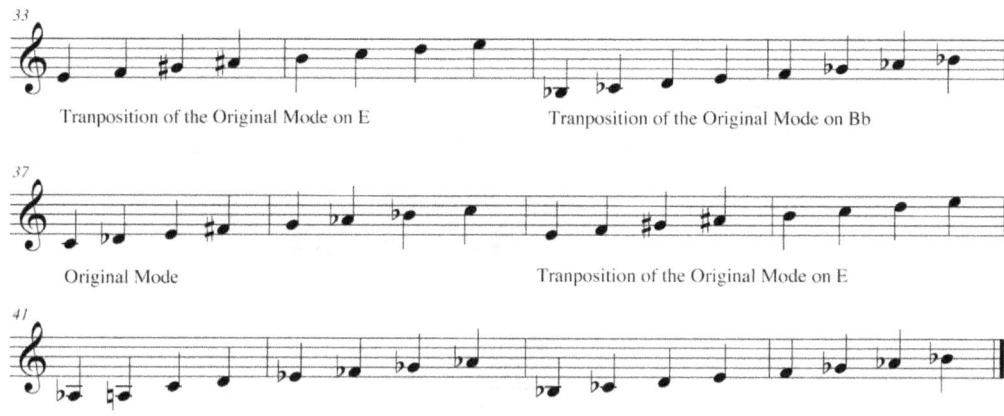

Tranposition of the Original Mode on E

Tranposition of the Original Mode on Bb

Original Mode

Tranposition of the Original Mode on E

Tranposition of the Original Mode on Ab

Tranposition of the Original Mode on Bb

Now I will superimpose the inverted generation a major second higher in the retrograde over the underlying chord progression of the same generation.

Im Folgenden werden die erzeugten Umkehrungen im Abstand einer großen Sekunde über die darunterliegende Akkordfolge desselben Tonmaterials geschichtet.

POLYMODAL MARRIAGE

EXAMPLE 81

Generated Mode #7 from E   E-F#-A-A#-C-D-D#

Generated Mode #6 from C   C-D-F-F#-G#-A#-B

Original Mode C-Db-E-F#-G-Ab-Bb

Generated Mode #5 from Bb   Bb-C-D#-E-F#-G#-A

Generated Mode #4 from Ab

Generated Mode #1 Gb-Ab-B-C-D-E-F

Ab-Bb-C#-D-E-F#-G

Generated Mode #2 Ab-Bb-C#-D-E-F#-G

This entire environment is polymodal however completely homogenous.

We can prepare through our controlled inversions a row of possible chords that can be utilized as a form of synthetic symmetry.

Die musikalische Umgebung, die durch diesen Vorgang geschaffen wird, ist polymodal, jedoch vollkommen homogen.

Durch geordnete Umkehrung lassen sich Akkorde herleiten, die als eine Art synthetische Symmetrie benutzt werden können.

POLYMODAL MARRIAGE PART 2

The exposition of these inversions has as well the effect of a musical unity and can be used to create as well a new modal generation through the methods discussed in Chapter 10. Each quadrad through inverted generation gives us the opportunity to create a further logical progression of modes. As discussed earlier each chord derived from inverted generation will serve as a matrix for this process.

Diese Umkehrungen bringen auch den Effekt einer musikalischen Einheit hervor und können, angewendet wie in Kapitel 10 beschrieben, eine neue modale Umgebung schaffen. Jeder durch Umkehrung erzeugte Vierklang ermöglicht weitere logische Akkordprogressionen und kann so als Matrix für weitere Prozesse dienen.

EXAMPLE 83

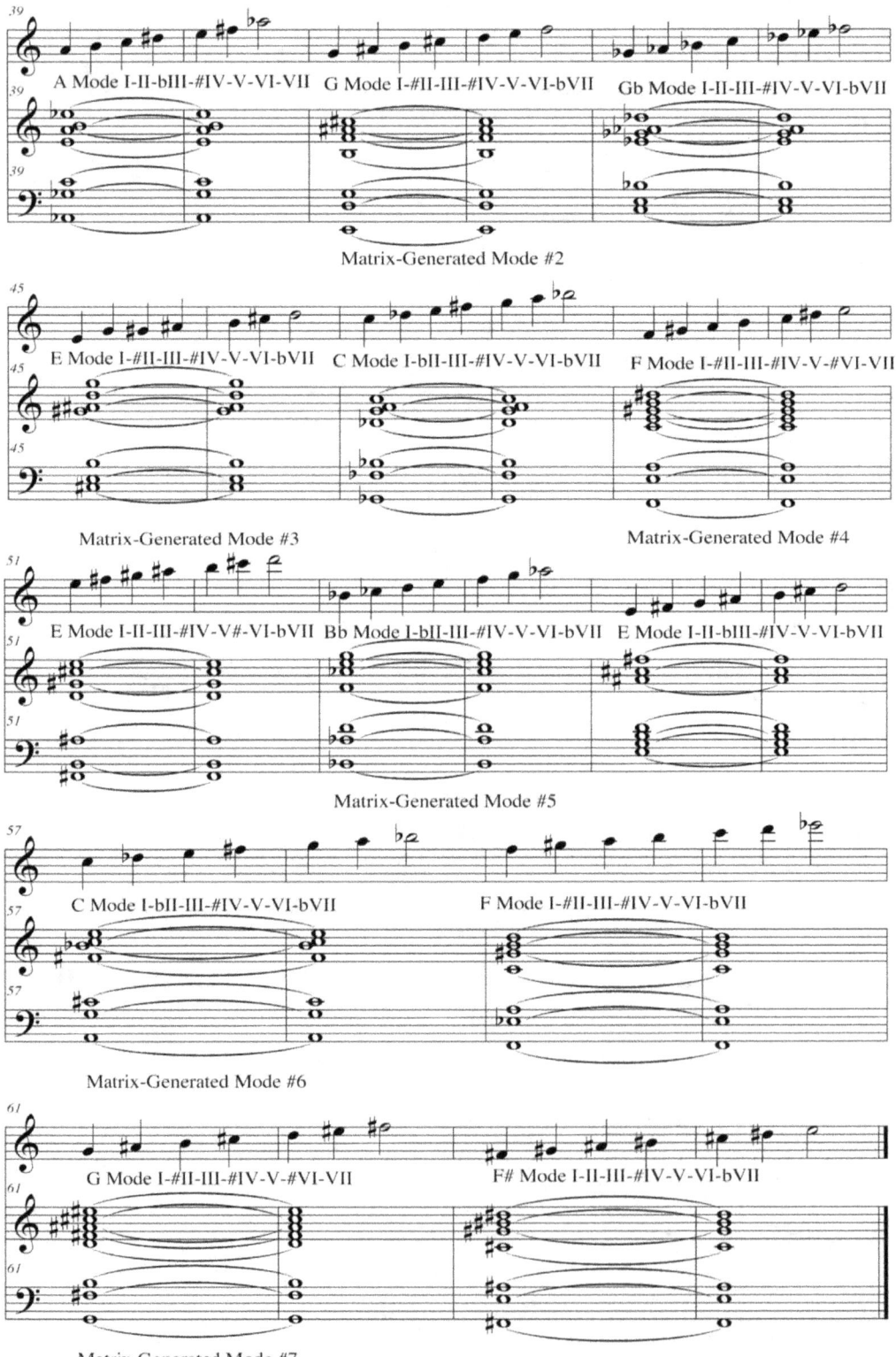

14) TONALITY and MODALITY

As we know traditional structural tonality, through the usage of the dominant seventh chord, has made use of the tritone as a modulatory device. With the application of secondary dominants we notice that we are actually patterning the movement of tritones.

14) TONALITÄT UND MODALITÄT

Bekanntlich macht sich die traditionelle Tonalität die modulatorischen Eigenschaften des Tritonus im Dominantseptakkord zunutze. Bei der Nutzung sekundärer Dominanten erkennt der aufmerksame Leser die Muster der Tritoni wieder.

EXAMPLE 84

During late Romanticism, Impressionism and in Jazz, with the advent of George Gershwin and Duke Ellington, the blending of modes with tonality began.

One can take a traditional harmonic movement and paint each chord with modal pitches.

In der Spätromantik, im Impressionismus und im Jazz mit George Gershwin und Duke Ellington begann die Verschmelzung von Modi und Dur-Moll-Tonalität. Um dies nachzuvollziehen, nehmen wir eine dur-moll-tonale Kadenzsequenz und betupfen jeden Akkord mit modalen Tönen.

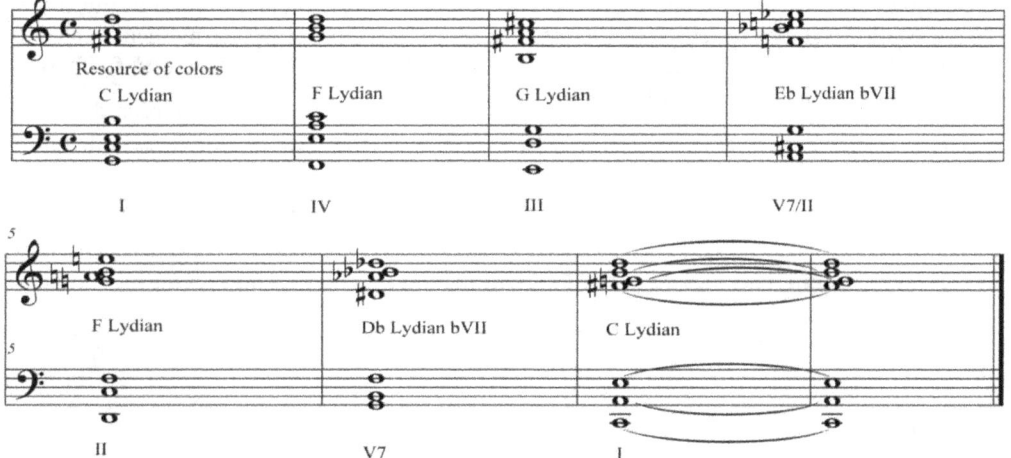

EXAMPLE 85

The interval after the "Lydian" means exactly this chromatical variation.
For example C Lydian bVII reads (C-D-E-#F-G-A-Bb)

For example each basic triad could receive four extra tones bringing about a seven-note environment. The function of the tritone in a row of secondary dominants will not change.

Zum Beispiel bekommt jeder Grund-Dreiklang vier weitere Optionen, was eine siebentönige Umgebung zum Ergebnis hat. Die Funktion des Tritonus in einer Folge Kadenzen mit sekundären Dominanten wird sich nicht verändern.

EXAMPLE 86

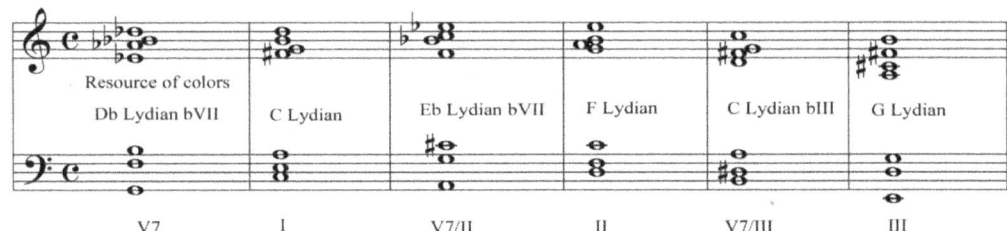

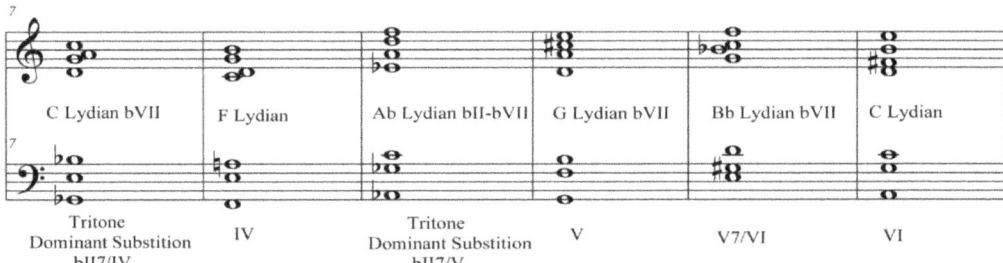

Later in Jazz John Coltrane Miles Davis and Thelonious Monk would freely move harmonies using various II-V-I resolutions. Modals color would enhance the chords and a logical tritonic movement came to be.

Später werden im Jazz John Coltrane, Miles Davis und Thelonious Monk Harmonien durch Gebrauch verschiedener II-V-I Auflösungen frei bewegen.

Die modalen Klangfarben werden den Sound der Akkorde steigern und eine logische Tritonusbewegung entsteht.

EXAMPLE 87

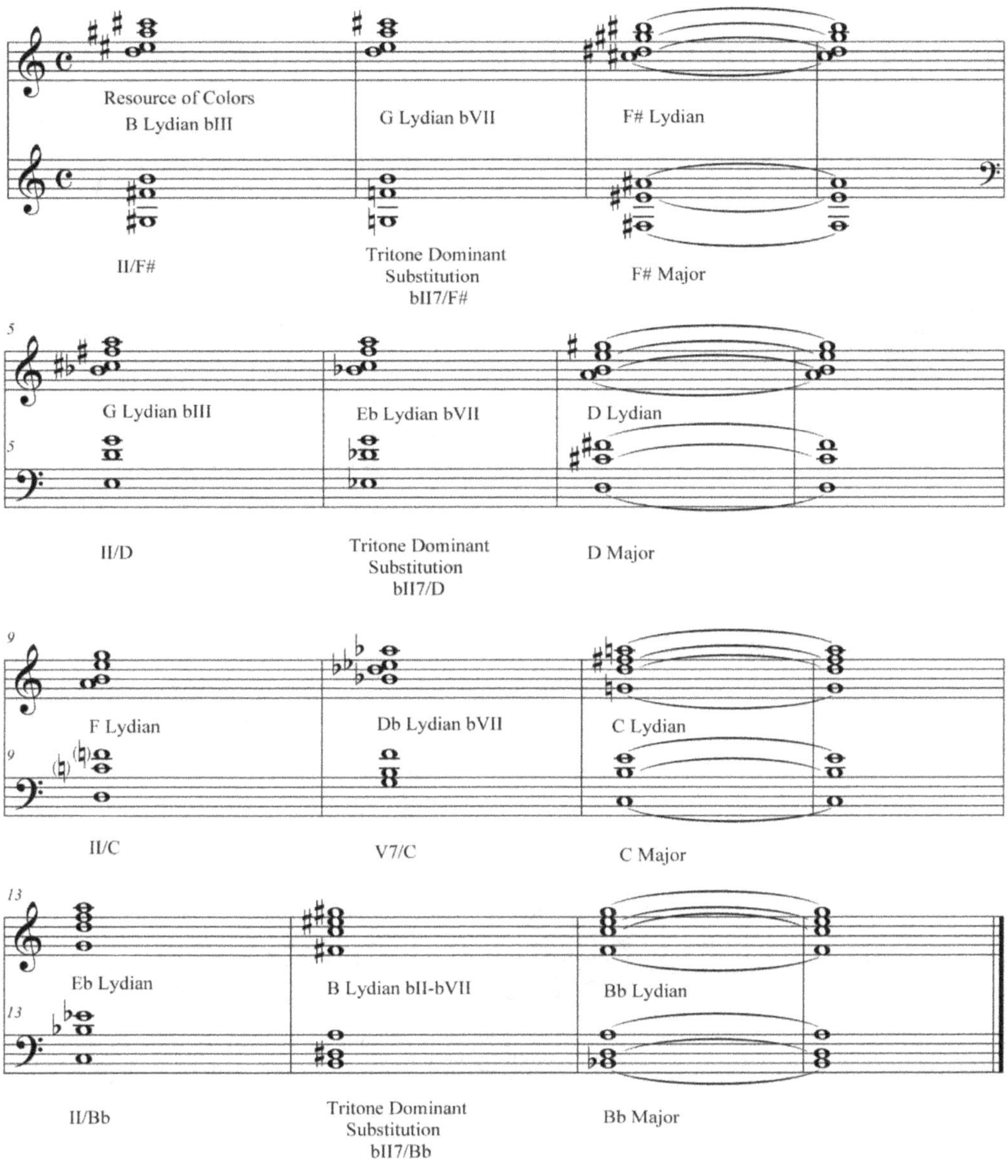

With tonal thinking we have, as well, all church modes for possible chordal substitution. When we translate these modes to the Ionic we have, when in C Major, the possibility of borrowing from Bb, Ab, G, F, Eb, and Db Major bringing a special form of extended tonality into music. Firstly I will exhibit a simple triadic progression.

Im tonalen Denken stehen uns alle Kirchenmodi weiterhin für Akkordfolgeerweiterungen zur Verfügung. Wenn wir diese Modi ins „Ionische" übersetzen, haben wir zum Beispiel in C-Dur die Möglichkeit, uns in B, Ab, G, F, Eb, und Des-Dur zu bedienen und dadurch eine besondere Form erweiterter Tonalität in die Musik einzubringen. Um dies zu veranschaulichen, zuerst eine einfache Progression von Dreiklängen:

152

MODAL TONAL

EXAMPLE 88

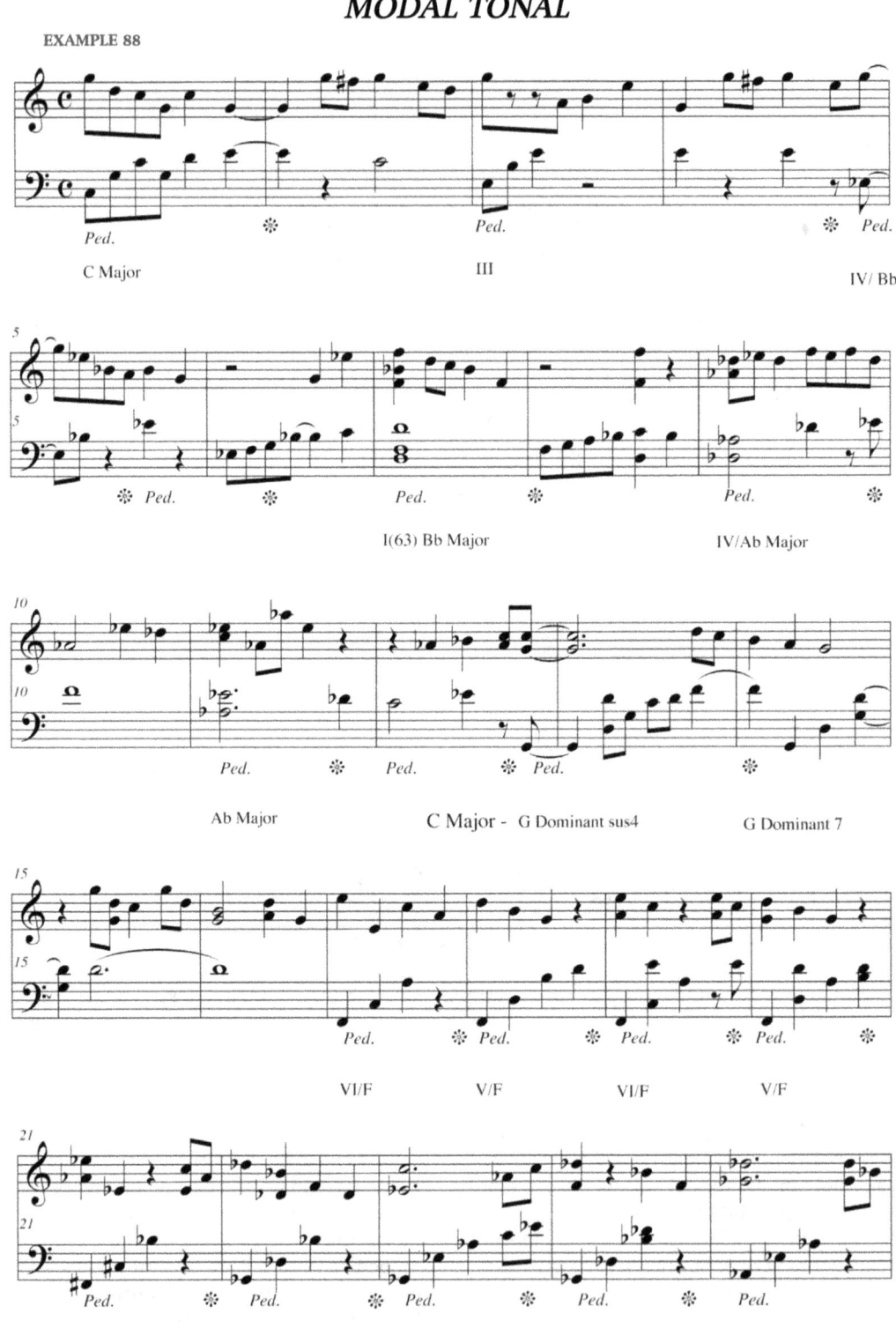

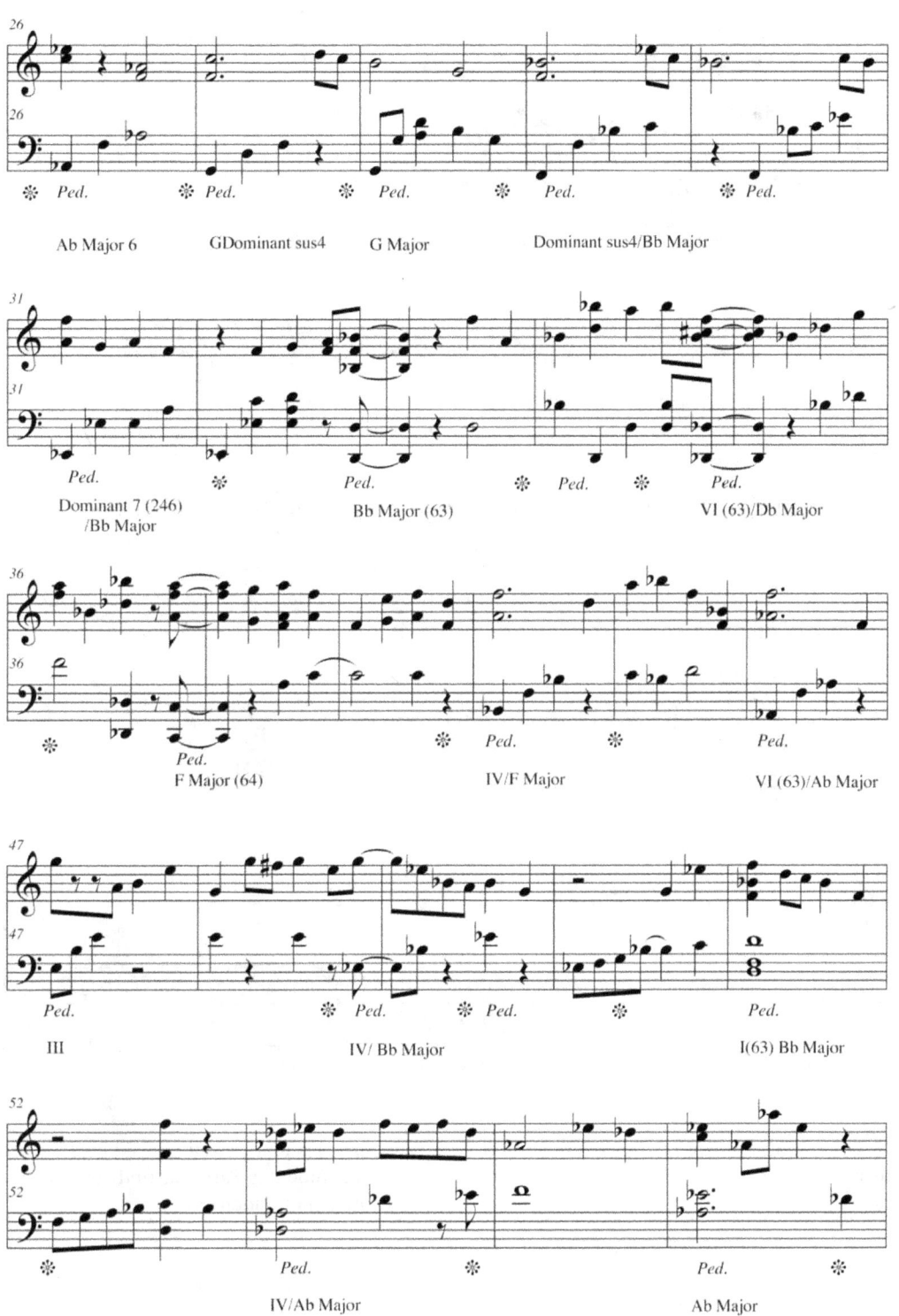

Now I will exhibit an extended progression with this technique using modal coloring and applying various cadences.

Als Nächstes eine erweiterte Akkordfolge mit der Technik modaler Färbung und der Anwendung verschiedener Kadenzen:

MODAL CADENZEN

The choice of which mode can be used is open. The triad must however be found within the modes one wishes to use for this coloristic effect. At the beginning of this musical direction various modes had been favoritized in the practice of this music. These are the following, the Lydian as a resource and the Lydian with a minor seventh or the overtone scale as a second resource.

Die Wahl der zu nutzenden Modi ist frei. Zwingend ist, dass der Dreiklang in dem Modus, den man für diesen Farbeffekt nutzen will, enthalten ist. Zu Beginn dieser Musikrichtung wurden verschiedene Modi für ihre praktische Umsetzung favorisiert. Diese sind der Lydische Modus als Hauptquelle und der Lydische mit kleiner Septime (auch die „Obertonskala" genannt).

EXAMPLE 90

BOP CADENZEN

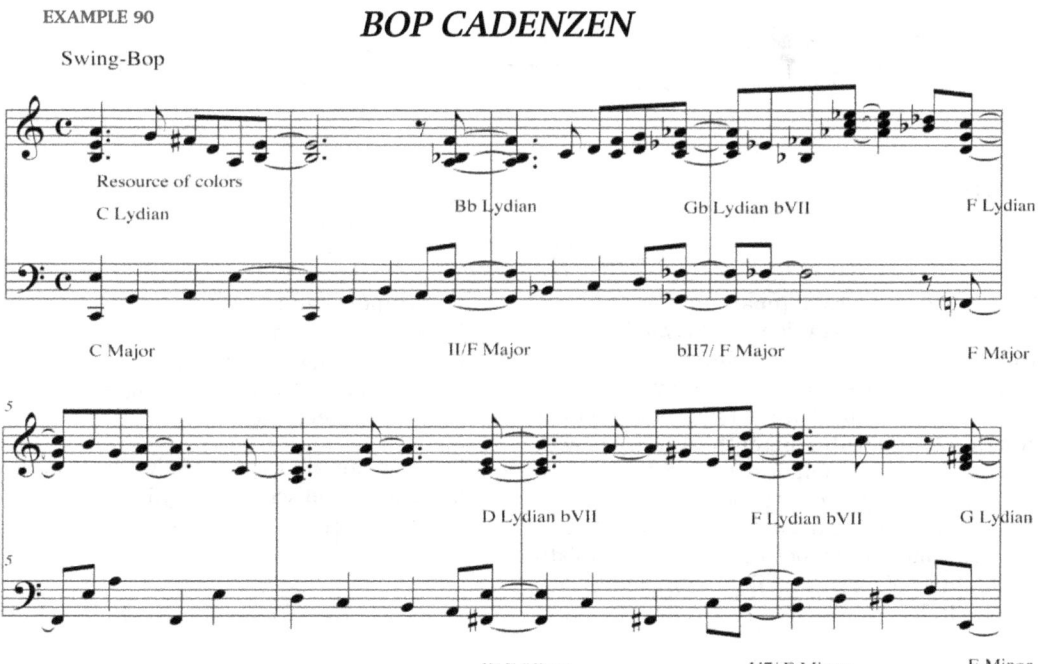

However we can expand tonal thinking with any mode in the thesaurus as long as this mode has the given triad or dominant seventh, (perhaps without the fifth) within itself. An example of some alternative modes could be the Lydian with a minor seventh, a Lydian with a minor third, a Lydian with a minor second and a minor seventh, a Lydian with an augmented second and a minor seventh, a Lydian with a minor third and a minor seventh, a Lydian with an augmented second and an augmented sixth or perhaps a Lydian with a minor third and an augmented sixth.

Im Grunde kann man tonales Denken mittels jedes Modus aus der Sammlung dieses Buches erweitern, solange diese Modi den Dreiklang oder Dominantseptakkord (eventuell auch ohne Quinte) in sich bergen.

Beispiele für alternative Modi wären: Lydisch b7, Lydisch b3, Lydisch b2 b7, Lydisch #2 b7, Lydisch b3 b7, Lydisch #2 #6 oder Lydisch b3 #6.

EXAMPLE 91

With heptatonic modes we will always have four pitches in which to color the original triad or dominant seventh chord. Here are some more adventurous combinations.

In heptatonischen Modi werden immer vier Töne da sein, um den Ursprungs-Dreiklang oder den Dominantseptakkord zu färben. Hier einige weitere abenteuerliche Kombinationen:

The relationship to the Church Modes is shifted in that this chord progression is in Minor. Therefore Eb is the Ionic instead of C.

MODAL CADENZEN PART 2

EXAMPLE 92

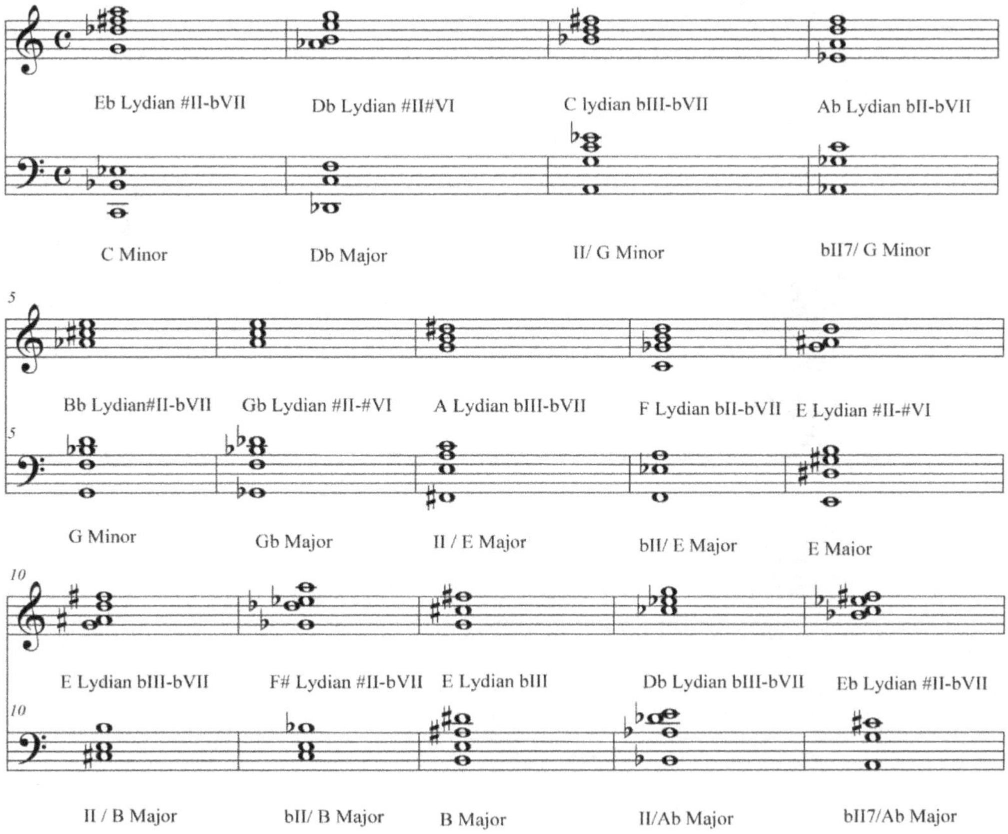

We can also apply larger modes if we wish and become very expansive creating complex tonal-modal structures and as well superimpose upon them as was discussed earlier.

Die Anwendung größerer Modi ist eine weitere Möglichkeit. Wir können komplexe tonal-modale Strukturen schaffen, auf die natürlich auch überlagert werden kann.

EXAMPLE 93

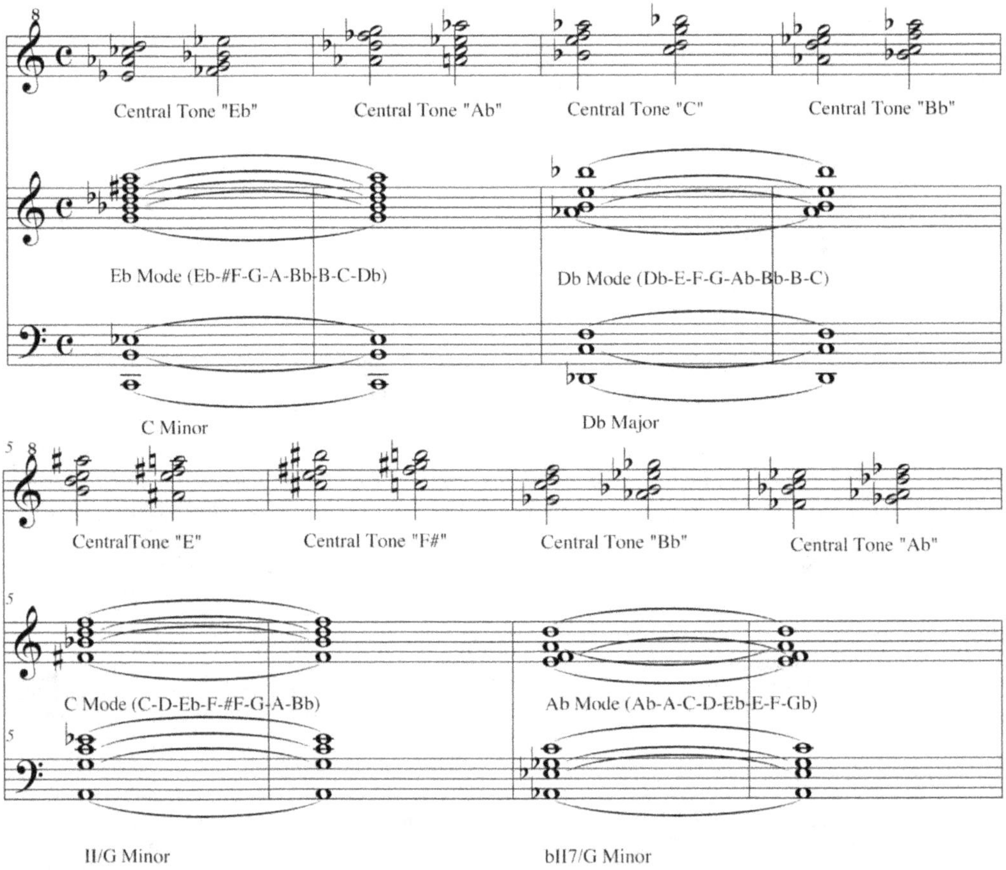

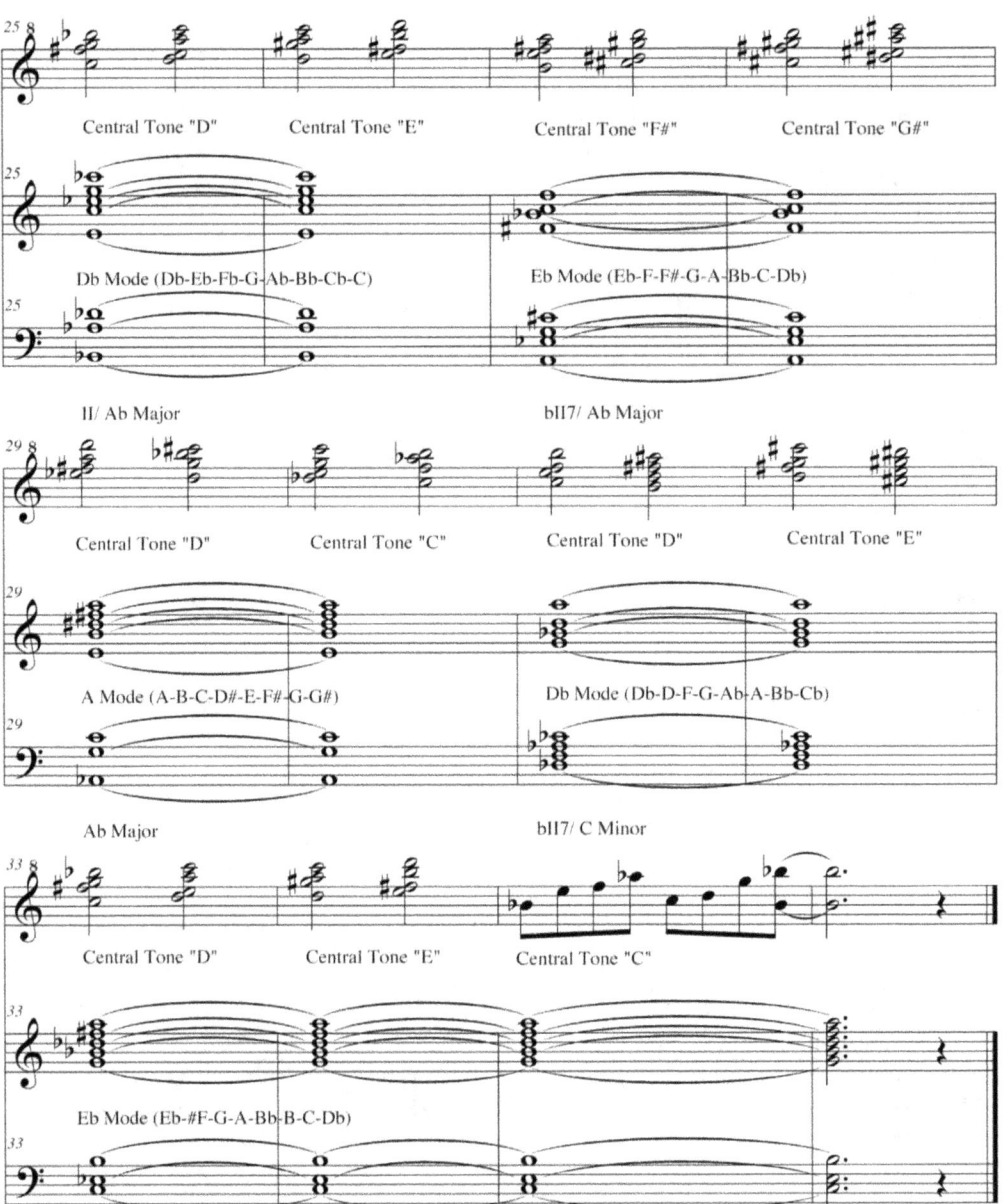

15) THE APPLICATION OF THE THEORY IN THE WORLD OF MICROTONICS

As we have seen one can distribute freely pitches around a given symmetrical axis and therewith construct modalities for possible transpositional schemes. With this basic principle we can of course free ourselves from our twelve-note division of an octave and bring the theory into full usage with other perfect divisions of an octave that precipitate other prime numerical symmetrical axes. Each of these symmetrical axes must be with the sum of its members a prime number (for example the tritone consisting of two members or the augmented triad which consists of three members.)

A microtonic division of the octave resulting in another prime numerical symmetrical axis could be for example, the number 15. With 15 notes equally dividing an octave we have the augmented triad as well as the symmetrical axis with a division of the number 5.

We can as well utilize this symmetrical axis as a nucleus and develop modes from the other 10 remaining pitches. Then one can use the 15 steps of this microtonal chromatical scale for a given transpositional scheme. We can even go back to even smaller divisions of an octave where perhaps other prime numerical symmetrical axes occur. An example could be 8, 9 or 10 perfect divisions of an octave.

At this point one can propose, within the spectrum of human perception, a choice of free pitches not necessarily being a part of a symmetrical 15 or 10 note division of an octave. We could have a well-tempered symmetrical tritone, or augmented triad or perhaps a geometrically prime numerical division of an octave as 5, 7, 9, 11, 13, etc.

Then we can distribute whatever tones we wish and pattern the transpositions upon these unsymmetrical tones and as well the chosen prime numerical symmetrical axis. I will now demonstrate the geometric possibilities creating various divisions of an octave.

2 Divisions = Tritone
3 Divisions = Augmented Triad
4 Divisions = 2 Tritones
5 Divisions = Pentatone
6 Divisions = 3 Tritones and 2 Augmented Triads
7 Divisions = Heptatone
8 Divisions = 4 Tritones
9 Divisions = 3 Augmented Triads
10 Divisions = 5 Tritones and 2 Pentatones
11 Divisions = Undecatone
12 Divisions = 6 Tritones and 4 Augmented Triads
13 Divisions = Tredecatone
14 Divisions = 7 Tritones and 2 Heptatones
15 Divisions = 5 Augmented Triads and 3 Pentatones
16 Divisions = 8 Tritones
17 Divisions = Septdecatone
18 Divisions = 9 Tritones, 6 Augmented Triads
19 Divisions = Nonedecatone
20 Divisions = 10 Tritones and 4 Pentatones
21 Divisions = 7 Augmented Triads and 3 Heptatones
22 Divisions = 11 Tritones and 2 Undecatones
23 Divisions = Ventetretone
24 Divisions = 12 Tritones and 8 Augmented Triads
25 Divisions = 5 Pentatones
26 Divisions = 13 Tritones and 2 Tredecatones
27 Divisions = 9 Augmented Triads
28 Divisions = 14 Tritones and 4 Heptatones
29 Divisions = Ventenonetone
30 Divisions = 15 Tritones 10 Augmented Triads and 6 Pentatones
31 Divisions = Trenteunotone
32 Divisions = 16 Tritones
33 Divisions = 11 Augmented Triads and 3 Undecatones
34 Divisions = 17 Tritones and 2 Septdecatones
35 Divisions = 5 Heptatones and 7 Pentatones
36 Divisions = 18 Tritones and 12 Augmented Triads

The human ear can decipher at the most 72 divisions of an octave.

Therefore I will not offer any further prime numerical divisions.

38 Divisions = 19 Tritones and 2 Nonedecatones
39 Divisions = 13 Augmented Triads and 3 Tredecatones
40 Divisions = 20 Tritones and 8 Pentatones
42 Divisions = 21 Tritones 14 Augmented Triads and 6 Heptatones
44 Divisions = 22 Tritones and 4 Undecatones
45 Divisions = 15 Augmented Triads and 9 Pentatones
46 Divisions = 23 Tritones and 2 Ventetretones
48 Divisions = 24 Tritones and 16 Augmented Triads
49 Divisions = 7 Heptatones
50 Divisions = 25 Tritones and 10 Pentatones
51 Divisions = 17 Augmented Triads and 3 Septdecatones
52 Divisions = 26 Tritones and 4 Tredecatones
54 Divisions = 27 Tritones and 18 Augmented Triads
55 Divisions = 11 Pentatones and 5 Undecatones
56 Divisions = 28 Tritones and 8 Heptatones
57 Divisions = 19 Augmented Triads and 3 Nonedecatones
58 Divisions = 29 Tritones and 2 Ventenonetones
60 Divisions = 30 Tritones and 20 Augmented Triads and 12 Pentatones
62 Divisions = 31 Tritones and 2 Trenteunotones
63 Divisions = 21 Augmented Triads and 9 Heptatones
64 Divisions = 32 Tritones
65 Divisions = 13 Pentatones and 5 Tredecatones
66 Divisions = 33 Tritones, 22 Augmented Triads and 6 Undecatones
68 Divisions = 34 Tritones and 4 Septdecatones
69 Divisions = 23 Augmented Triads and 3 Ventetretones
70 Divisions = 35 Tritones 14 Pentatones and 10 Heptatones
72 Divisions = 36 Tritones and 24 Augmented Triads

www.ingramcontent.com/pod-product-compliance
Lightning Source LLC
Chambersburg PA
CBHW080224170426
43192CB00015B/2748